24 HOURS TO THE PERFECT INTERVIEW

Quick Steps for Planning, Organizing, and Preparing for the Interview that Gets the Job

Matthew J. DeLuca
& Nanette F. DeLuca

McGraw-Hill

New York   Chicago   San Francisco
Lisbon   London   Madrid   Mexico City
Milan   New Delhi   San Juan   Seoul
Singapore   Sydney   Toronto

1 2 3 4 5 6 7 8 9 0   AGM/AGM   0 1 0 9 8 7 6 5 4

ISBN 0-07-142403-2

McGraw-Hill books are available at special quantity discounts to use as premiums and sales promotions, or for use in corporate training programs. For more information, please write to the Director of Special Sales, McGraw-Hill Professional, Two Penn Plaza, New York, NY 10121-2298. Or contact your local bookstore.

 This book is printed on recycled, acid-free paper containing a minimum of 50% recycled, de-inked fiber.

CONTENTS

Contents

ACKNOWLEDGMENTS

We wish to thank Gary Wong from *job-interview.net,* who has continued to provide us with a platform to interact with job seekers on a worldwide basis. This interaction has enabled us to keep a finger on the pulse of job seekers—in this ever-challenging job market—and their most immediate concerns while we answer their urgent questions directly and provide content for the Web site.

Others to whom we wish to express our appreciation include Sue Winters and Nancy Jackman from the Winmar Personnel Agency. They show repeatedly what true recruiting professionals offer to both corporate clients and job seekers. We also wish to thank Steve Dimowitz, Ellen Perlstein, and Sara Sternberg, at The Ayers Group, a most generous, multifaceted HR consulting firm for offering their suggestions, unique expertise, inspiring and creative insights, and hospitality during the writing of this book. Last, we would like to thank Carol DeDominico from Lee Hecht Harrison and Bobbie Lyons at Right Management Associates, who are always willing to give time and attention to those who are looking for their next career opportunity and have so much skill and expertise to offer.

We would be remiss if we neglected to name three others—all with outstanding skill sets and talent who either directly or indirectly contributed to the inspiration for this book. They are Jonathan Opas of Human Resource Staffing Solutions, a unique organization that seems to have a big heart and is really willing to make long-term commitments to people. Then there is Marcia Pollard, a real cheerleader who is a terrific person to work with and has a great career to look forward to. The third person we want to mention is Gilen Chan. She always finds time to provide insight and direction to a variety of projects and activities along with the people connected to them, as busy as she is with her own very senior position at Grey Advertising.

Finally, let us also mention that yet another book for McGraw-Hill was made possible due to the continuing belief of Phillip Ruppel and Donya Dickerson that others want to hear what we have to say.

INTRODUCTION

All those emails, all those letters you have sent, all those resumes mailed, and all those "networking" opportunities were all done with one goal in mind—for you to get the interview that will get you the job!

It is a very simple axiom: no interviews, no job offers.

So which of these scenarios seems the most familiar to you?

- You have diligently sent out targeted cover letters with your resume—now you find a response on the answering machine when you come back with your morning papers.

- A friend of a friend has given you a "hot" lead for a job that seems ideal—you need to follow up today.

- You have been spreading the word, networking wisely, and "rrring"—you get a telephone call at 9:15 this morning for an interview tomorrow.

- Checking your usual online sources, you have been sending your resume to several posting sites; this morning's e-mail finds a positive response. They want to meet with you as soon as possible.

- You have been complaining for months to anyone who would listen how you "have to get another job;" finally, someone listened and here is a great job opening, but you have to act fast.

What will you do next? What can you do? What should you not do?

- Given that this interview looming on the horizon might be "the" one to get you that long-awaited job offer.

- Given that this might be your "one-shot" chance for this job.

- Given that time is of the essence—you might only have 24 hours until "showtime."

You have to do the right thing right now! And this book will teach you everything you need to know to prepare in the short time you have before the interview.

What is your game plan for this interview? Do you have a plan?

What kind of interview will it be: in person, over the telephone, a group interview, or serial interviews?

Why is this interview important to you? Why do you want it? And why do you want this particular job—or do you?

3 Rs of Interviewing

Whether you have 24 hours or 24 days to prepare, there are three simple steps to prepare for each and every interview.

1. Research
   - Yourself: your skills, experience, interests, success stories, aspirations, weaknesses, goals.
   - The organization: what they do, how they do it, their location, financial health, competitors, history, culture, management.
   - The industry: which industry they are involved in, the current situation in that industry, prognosis for the industry, what factors affect the industry—positively/negatively?

2. Rehearse
   - Know the facts about your experience, your skills, the job requirements, the organization, and the industry. Have them comfortably in mind. Practice aloud your answers to the questions you hope you will be asked; practice more answers to the ones you fear you will be asked.
   - Prepare your "look" for the interview.
   - Complete your last-minute checklist.

3. Relax
   - If you have done steps 1 and 2, then you have taken charge of those factors that you can control. Be confident that you are a candidate that can add great value

How Did You Get This Interview?

Referral? From whom?

Answered ad?

Print? Where? When?

Online? Source?

Other ads?

Recruiter?

Cold call? Mailing?

Figure I-1

quickly to their organization, and you can tell them exactly how and why!

To remove the mystique from the interview process, remember that an interview is just a conversation with a purpose. A conversation implies a "give and take," a sharing of ideas and viewpoints. What is the purpose of this particular conversation? It can differ from interview to interview, from interviewer to interviewer, and from what you want to get from the interview.

In order to know what you want, there are key questions you should ask yourself. Are you testing the waters—seeing if there is a market for your skills? Seeing if you can move to a different location? Concerned that your own position might be eliminated and are trying to stay one step ahead? Is this your planned "next step" on your long-term career path? Are you presently unemployed and growing depressed as your funds dwindle down to fumes?

Knowing what you want and what you can offer is a huge part of preparing for any interview. If you were selling cars, you would be expected to have a wealth of information for the customer. You would know about the various features, including maintenance requirements and performance capability and its actual track record. Rather than selling a car, you are selling yourself, and you should be conversant with all your main selling points.

Always Be Prepared

If you have been actively searching for a job, you should have a basic level of preparation already present. It is important to always be in a state of readiness for an interview because mini-interviews can take place at any time, in any place. That person seated next to you at dinner might have a job opening. When you drop your children off at school, the parent you grab a cup of coffee with might have an important contact for you. Elevator conversations could lead somewhere. Having attained a basic level of preparedness allows you to kick yourself up a notch!

As part of the job search process, you need to *learn* about yourself in sufficient terms to *sell* yourself. You also need to know about the organizations, the industries, and the jobs where you seek employment. Putting those two knowledge bases together answers the all-important question: *"Why should we hire you?"*

It is becoming a cliché to warn of the hundreds—or thousands—of resumes submitted for every job. Resumes arrive by mail, electronically, by fax, and even slipped under the door! Just wading through all those resumes is a huge task, so if yours has risen to the surface and you are contacted for an interview, it is like winning a minilottery. You cannot jeopardize or squander this opportunity. It might be several months before you get another!

Organizations of every size and composition must pay particular attention to their bottom lines, as should every employee and job candidate. Globalization, the worldwide and local economic roller-coaster, the aging "baby boomers," and technological imperatives have constantly changed both the workforce and the workplace. We all have had to shift gears in many areas of our daily lives in the past year or two. But, with all the technology, with all the changes, the basics of getting a job offer remain the ubiquitous interview process.

So the first order of business in this book is to get the interview! The next step is to use the proven techniques provided in this book to maximize your opportunities in the interview and get the job offer! (See Figure I-1.)

Note: At the end of each chapter, we have included "Last-Minute Checklists." No matter how much time you have available to prepare, read these. If you have more time to prepare, read through the entire book, spending more time in each area.

Getting Ready

CHAPTER ONE

Setting Up the Interview

Let's start by congratulating you if, in fact, you are reading this book because you have an interview to go to within a very short time—perhaps within the next 24 hours. Whenever you get an interview (face to face certainly, but credit is due even for a phone interview), you should be quite pleased with yourself for the following reasons:

1. You got through. Research shows that today it takes at least eight attempts to get through to a specific person for an actual contact to occur. This includes those simple issues such as approval to pay an invoice or to ask a quick question about getting an interview.
2. To land a job in this market, statistics show that you will probably need at least eight specific job opportunities before you are successful and obtain a job offer. This means that you have to have been considered as a possible candidate for eight different positions!
3. Recent research also indicates that you are going to need 20–24 prospects and real contacts before you successfully complete your search.
4. The best time to go on the offensive is when you are seeing signs of success in your efforts—such as getting called in for an interview, even on short notice.

What did you do to successfully land the interview? What can you do to sharpen those skills and increase your success rate? Despite all the technology and electronic gadgets and devices, the way that continues to be the best way by far for a person to get a job is through the interview process. In today's very challenging job market, interviewing is being used more rather than less, and more follow-up interviews are being required before any job offers are made.

In fact, it is not unusual to hear that some organizations require 10 to 15 interviews before making a final decision. Therefore, this book will help you prepare not only for the first courtesy or screening interview, but also for the interviews that follow.

Why Do You Want the Interview?

What made you do it? What was there about the ad? Who tipped you off to the job opening? Be certain with just 24 hours to go that you have a clear idea of not only your objective, but of theirs as well.

What Is the Reason to Seek an Interview?

- *First*, for a job.
- If that is not a possibility, the *second* reason is to obtain an interview for job leads.
- The *third* reason for an interview is to obtain information.

That's it. There should be no other reasons, and any other interviews will take time away from your obtaining a job. If you are without a job and if you are in Human Resources, for example, you easily could spend all of your time interviewing, but there is no guarantee that any of that effort will lead to employment. Effort is needed to find a job, but there is no rule that says for spending X amount of effort you then have a right to expect to be offered a job. (See Figure 1-1.)

What do you think the other person is hoping to gain from agreeing to meet with you? It is very important for you to consider the person you will meet with to determine what it is that made them agree to the meeting and what he hopes to accomplish.

Recently there was an unemployed HR executive in New York City who happened to mention to a friend of his that he had just lost his job, who then shared the information with his wife, a bank officer that deals with employee retirement plans. She, without hesitation, asked for his resume and before long the jobless individual received a phone call from one of the bank's clients calling to set up an interview. This was exciting news because he was having very little success from a variety of techniques he was using to obtain interviews. He was careful to warn himself that due to the nature of the relationship, this was probably only a courtesy interview. Because the location of the employer was more than 100 miles away, his friends and family were raising questions about how he could even consider working at such a distance. He had thoughtfully considered a "what if" scenario but did not give it much thought because he suspected the meeting would be a courtesy. So

Why Do an Interview?

Your reasons:

- You need a job—soon.
- You need a job —any job—right now.
- You need a lead on a real job opening.
- You want to see if there are better jobs than the one you have.
- You want to see if you can make more money elsewhere.
- You are testing the market.
- You need some information about the industry or job opening.
- Someone suggested you "talk" to them for career guidance.

Their reasons:

- They need to fill a vacancy—soon. Maybe.
- They need to fill a vacancy—now. Yesterday.
- They have several candidates in mind and want to see more.
- They know who they want to hire and just want to prove that he/she is the best out there.
- They heard it is a buyer's market and they should see many, many applicants for each position.
- They need to show they tried to fill position for EEOC standards.
- They are "going through the motions" for internal, political reasons.
- They were told to see you by someone with some clout. There is no job opening. Or there might be.
- They were asked to see you as a favor. There is no job opening. Or there might be.

Figure 1-1

off he went to meet a senior member of the organization in the recruiting unit, and they had a terrific conversation. The interviewer made some strong statements about how something appropriate was about to open up and asked if the HR pro would be interested. "Absolutely," he stated without hesitation, knowing that this is said more often than not in a similar way to "Let's have lunch," without any real intent at closure. To prove the point, a few days after the meeting and after writing a thank-you letter, the applicant placed a call to the interviewer, who would not take his call, and he has not heard from the interviewer since.

The reason for this story is to demonstrate that when you go on an interview, you should determine its purpose in advance. Now, had he known that his instincts were correct, would the HR pro have been better off passing on the meeting? He did not think so for two reasons. First, he wanted to show appreciation to his friend and his wife for taking the initiative, and second, his instinct might have been wrong. In addition, because he was not getting any other invitations at that point, he had an opportunity to demonstrate, practice, and evaluate his interview skills so he would be better prepared when a "real" opportunity presented itself.

A far better practice when you are looking for a job is to try to accept only those meetings where there is a real and specific job under consideration. Maximizing your time and energy is an essential element of any effective job search. It is too easy to become distracted and lose focus —with not just hours but days and weeks quickly dissipating as activities are pursued that yield no results.

To continue this point, let's review how you got the interview. This is important to remember because you need to see what is working and what isn't. The key to success is trying and retrying a mix of different approaches. One way to reduce your chances of getting an interview is to spend all your time on the Internet. It is great that you are sending out 20 e-mails daily (with latest resume attached). And it's just peachy that you religiously change your resume on Monster weekly so that it pops up as new when prospective employers scan the Web for potential candidates

As scary as it sounds,—all those efforts might well be for naught. Although more jobs are increasingly obtained through Internet sources, most recent research indicates that the success rate is still just in single digits. In fact, 5 percent is the most recent number mentioned.

The point is if you get your interview from the Internet—great. If you obtained it from some other more traditional source, that's fine too and more likely.

Regardless of the source, keep track of your successes from all sources so that you will be able to continually refine your search by spending more time and energy with those sources that have been leading to successful results. As you will see below, if you keep the big picture in mind, you will concentrate without distraction on those avenues that lead to results and interviews.

Getting the Interview

So how do you get interviews? Any way you can, and be ready because you never know when the call will come. The rest of this chapter discusses proven ways to land that all-important interview.

The 80-20 Rule, and Then Some

Before you start the process of setting up an interview, there is a great rule to keep in mind: Pareto's principle. It applies in this situation to an extreme. In one of its universal applications (and the one that we are using here), the rule states that you get 80 percent of your results from 20 percent of your activity. The more you identify where you are getting your best results, the more likely your efforts will turn into additional successful results. Examine what led you to this interview, and focus more on that activity because it's proven to be the most fruitful. (See Figures 1-2 and 1-3.)

Your Investment

Consider also the time invested when you actually succeed and are invited for an interview. First, there are the three Rs of preparation—Research, Rehearse, Relax—all representing an investment of time. Do not discount your personal preparation time (haircut, dry cleaning, choosing outfit), travel time, and the actual time spent in the interview and recording notes afterwards.

You will also need to devote time to the follow-up process and sending a thank you. One creative person we know is sending $5 Starbucks gift certificates (*to "have a cup of coffee on him"*) with the thank-you note, as a sign of appreciation for the meeting. Don't forget to follow-up and call when asked to do so.

How Did You Get This Interview?

Referral? From whom?

Answered ad?

      Print? Where? When?

      Online? Source?

      Other ads?

Recruiter?

Cold call? Mailing?

Figure 1-2

Getting Your Foot in the Door

To get a job interview, you need to identify the organizations that have openings that you are qualified to fill. Armed with this information, you then need to determine your best entry point or contact person. Consider anyone who is the most likely to get you the interview so you could demonstrate your value. Consider anyone who can serve, if not as the person with the authority to hire, as least as a "passer-on" (the opposite of a "gatekeeper" who tries to screen out). You are looking for the person who can screen you in. This could be a friend, a neighbor, a relative, or even a parent of a friend of your kids from school.

If none of these is an option, then you might consider making a cold call. The coldest of calls occurs when you pick up the phone or show up in person unannounced and request a meeting. A better approach is a marketing letter with your resume attached that serves as your introduction and closes with a promise of a phone call from you on a specific date to set up a meeting. This approach seems to be more effective than pure cold calling, but the only evidence is from hearsay. (See Figure 1-4.)

When you send such a letter, remember to close with "I will call you on (insert day, for example, Monday) to set up a mutually

Path to Interviews and Interviews That Lead to a Job

Identify organizations that have the jobs.
  Identify organizations that have job openings.
    Identify job openings that match my skills.
      Identify hiring manager to contact.
        Send hiring manager resume and targeted marketing letter.
      Follow-up telephone call to hiring manager.
    More Follow-up telephone calls.
  Speak to hiring manager.
Get invited for interview.
  Prepare for interview.
    Ace the interview.
      Follow-up after interview.
      Additional follow-up.
      BINGO!
      Get job offer.
        Negotiate job offer.
      Accept job offer.
    Start new job.
    Enjoy new job.

Figure 1-3

convenient meeting." You might even choose to add, "I am confident it will be well worth your time." Just remember to make the call on the day you promised you would; many people do not. To increase the certainty that your message reaches the eyes of your intended, consider sending an e-mail if you can get the address. The reason is because the higher up the person is in the organization, the less likely your intended receiver will open his/her own mail, so your letter may never be even seen by him/her. With e-mail, there is still no such thing as the 100-percent guarantee, but there is more likelihood that s/he will be the one to open it.

Regardless of the strength of your contact (even if you have none), all attempts to obtain an interview should be directed to someone that you target in the organization. Department

Cold-Call Marketing Letter

Letterhead
(sent to Marketing Department Head)

Date

Name, Title
Organization
Address
City, State Zip

Dear Mr./Ms./Mrs./Dr. :

As a graphic artist I have admired your innovative packaging designs, particularly the new _____ recently introduced. It appeals to those who deplore waste in packaging materials while providing an appealing, eye-catching opportunity to sell the product.

For the past ___ years I have been the head of a small design firm located in ___ but am recently planning to relocate to your area.

Some of our clients that I worked with closely are _____. I have taken the liberty to enclose both my resume and a small photo portfolio of my recent work.

I will be in town the week of _____, and I will telephone you to set up a mutually convenient meeting to discuss my possible employment.

Sincerely,

Signature

Figure 1-4

heads, Human Resource professionals, the CEO are all possibilities. Do not send a "to whom it may concern" letter. It will not be taken seriously next to letters from other job seekers who took the time to find a specific contact name. And, if possible, avoid anonymous e-mail addresses (including *careers@xyzcorp. com*) because chances are your effort will fall into a bottomless electronic hole.

There is no excuse for being unable to find the most appropriate person to receive your resume. It takes effort and focus—two attributes every employer values!

Leads

You never know where the best lead is going to come from, so keep your network open by getting out and staying in touch. You need to be out and about, talking to people, meeting with your peers, being involved in your industry. Conventions, conferences, seminars are all ripe for leads. If it is not a secret that you are seeking employment, tell your friends and relatives. You never know who knows someone who knows someone else who has heard of a job opening. Your job search should not be your only subject of conversation, but many people like to be asked to help, to be thought of as someone with "the right contacts." Just do not be a drudge about it.

With Whom Should You Interview?

The best answer is, frankly, "Anyone who is willing to meet with you."

This is not a sarcastic remark and does not contradict what we said previously about conserving your resources. When we say meet with anyone willing to meet with you, we mean at those organizations you have already researched as being viable targets (they have jobs that you can and want to do, and there is a high probability of job openings if not specific knowledge of a definite vacancy right now). (See Figure 1-5.)

Do not automatically rule out anyone even if they are part of the contracted maintenance staff or someone's assistant. Those people might very well have clout and organizational knowledge, and their credibility might be very helpful in securing your objective. An additional incentive for them might be the opportunity to receive a referral award.

Whom to See for an Interview

Start at the top, work your way down

•

Highest person in the organizational structure

•

Person who would be your immediate supervisor or his/her boss.

•

Someone in authority from Human Resources

•

Any fans that might be helpful

Figure 1-5

Finally, if you know no one, try to find a receptive person, which often can be done with the help of a friendly, knowledgeable receptionist. Try calling the general number, and in a rehearsed presentation try to obtain information from the receptionist about who is the best person to talk to for a job that you understand is available in a specific department.

If the receptionist is not helpful, try calling when his/her replacement is there. If you are calling between 12:00 and 1:00, try next time between 1:00 and 2:00 to catch her replacement on lunchtime break.

How Do You Find Out Who Is in Charge?

Now you might say that all the above is fine, but I would always prefer to meet with the person in charge. How do you find out who is in charge? Who is making the hiring decision?

Depending on the level of what being "in charge" means, the higher up you go to look, the easier it is to find out.

- **Public information**—If the organization is publicly traded or governmental or not for profit, go to the source, namely the organization itself, and its Web site and promotional material, you will readily learn the names and titles of the persons at the highest level of the organization.

- **Secondary sources**—To obtain information about employees lower in the organizational hierarchy, you need to consider additional sources of information, including Internet search engines, such as Google, as well as friends, relatives, employees, and former employees. For some professions, trade groups and directories—hard copy and electronic—might be readily available.

- **Third-level sources**—At this level, to obtain correct names and titles, contact the organization yourself, preferably by phone. If all you have is the general number, when a voice answers, ask to be connected to the ABC department. Once in the ABC department, ask the voice for the correct spelling and title of the senior-most person's name. Ask also for the direct dial extension while you are at it. It does not hurt to ask. If they refuse to provide it, at least you tried.

An increasingly difficult challenge is to get any voice in any organization that will be responsive. The fine old custom of organizational life that allowed you to expect to always hear a knowledgeable person at the other end of the phone when you called the general (or main) telephone number is constantly being tested. Some organizations have gone to call center arrangements for all calls from outside the organization. Others have gone to automated response systems with elaborate menus that occasionally will never allow you to reach a human voice in the organization without specific knowledge of the extension of the person you are trying to call. Even in the case of the most advanced electronic systems, you will be able to find the information you want, but you need to be patient and courteous in order to be effective and allow it to happen.

Two more alternatives are to contact the public relations arm of the organization you are trying to reach; another is the mail services area; and two other alternatives outside the organization are their vendors or suppliers and alumni lists that provide current affiliations and contact information.

How to Get the Interview? Ask for It!

If you want to set up an interview for yourself, you must ask for it. It all is related to what you do and do not have control over.

Barring an outright rude or confrontational response, it never hurts to ask for a meeting. Even if the request is turned down, you know what the answer is! Most people who say no to a request from you are more willing to agree to a second request. So after turning down your request for a meeting, they might provide names of a couple of people for you to contact instead.

As you will find when we discuss negotiations in Chapter 16, if you do not ask for something, you will never get it. The more you try by asking, the easier it will come. So start asking today.

You Get the Call!

After pursuing all those leads, the HR person at your dream company calls to set up an interview. You do have a professional-sounding message on your answering machine in case you are not there when "the" call comes through, correct? Do family members know what type of information to relay if it is a business call? (*"Mommy is sleeping" or "Daddy is mowing the lawn"* are not the best ways to answer inquiries.)

You take the call yourself and, of course, you have a notepad and listing of recent ads you have answered handy. Get the basic information:

- What is the name of the organization?
- What is the job opening?
- Where is job located?
- Where and when is interview?
- Whom will interview be with?
- Will others be present in interview?
- Directions? Floor/room number?

Write the information down. Refer to your calendar. It is a good practice to have your calendar and a notepad near the phone for just these occasions. Avoid having to reschedule at all costs —to have to do so gives the impression that you are either disorganized or you do not have as much control over your life as is preferred. Either or both might be false assumptions, but why even take that risk? (It is a good idea if there is a time gap between when the appointment was made and the actual appointment. That way, you can confirm a morning appointment the day before, and confirm an afternoon appointment that morning.

The appointment is set, so now it's time to get ready. First, let's be sure you remember to relax and enjoy the interview.

Enjoy the Interview?

Of course. It is about your favorite subject, the one you are the expert on: YOU. Other than being unavoidable to get jobs, what is good about the interview process? Think about it. This is the prime opportunity for you to do the following:

- **Discover yourself.** This process is the perfect opportunity for you to learn what your strengths and weaknesses are and to collect countless success stories from your past work and educational experiences. Your career might have taken surprising turns in the past, and more surprises might be open to you in the future.

- **Discover some great organizations.** Even if you are not offered a job, you will have learned something about different industries, organizations, and ways of doing business; you never know when this will come in handy in the future. Knowledge should always be appreciated.

- **Discover some really great people**. Additions to your professional networking database should not be ignored; NEVER close any doors. Each interviewer can teach you something about the process, about yourself. Even poor interviewers can teach you to appreciate the good ones!

(See Figure 1-6.)

Last-Minute Checklist

Why would anyone want to interview you?

☐ You could be a solution to their problems.

☐ You could add value to the organization.

☐ They have nothing else to do.

☐ They have a "quota" of candidates to see.

☐ Respect for your referral.

☐ Just a nice person; cannot say "no."

☐ No openings now but always on the lookout for good hires.

☐ *"Should I know you?" "Are you someone who can help me?"*

☐ Flattered that you think they are powerful.

☐ Rewarded for referrals.

Figure 1-6

CHAPTER TWO

Getting the Perfect Look

When it comes to how you should look for your job interview, the easiest rule to follow is to look like you already work there!

- Your resume should have the *targeted* experiences, skills, and qualities that literally paint you into the job. Your marketing (cover) letter should specifically address *that one job* at *that one organization*.

- Your dress, demeanor, and passion for the job should make the interviewer "see" you perfectly in the position.

Make it easy for the organization to select you; stand out from the other candidates with your preparation, skills, experience, enthusiasm, and your understanding of the organization's needs, but do not differ too greatly from the employee profile and culture the organization has built. (See Figure 2-1.)

Your Perfect Look

The Virtual You
> Resume
> Cover Letter
> References
> Work Samples

The Professional You
> Training and education
> Experience
> Skills
> Information
> Disclosure

The Physical You
> Dress
> Demeanor
> Voice
> Tone

Virtual You + Professional You + Physical You = CONSISTENCY

Figure 2-1

The Virtual You

What Statement Does Your Resume Make?

Is your resume a well-organized, accurate (no typos or mis-spellings), professional "snapshot" of you? Does it read like it was written just for this job at this organization? Was your cover letter really a marketing letter, written just for the specific company you are interviewing with, highlighting exactly what you want (an interview to get a particular job) and why you are the ideal candidate (you are a solution to their problems)? If your original resume was not all that it could be, the situation is still correctable: You will bring extra copies of your "updated" resume to the interview.

Secondly, if your cover letter was lacking in some areas, that too is correctable with a targeted telephone call to secure the interview itself, followed up by an excellent interview!

The Use of the Word "Targeted" Is Deliberate

To have a target, you set your sights on a particular end and focus effort to attain it. An archer is not distracted; she knows what the job at hand is—to get the arrow into the center of the bull's-eye! Your resume and cover letter are the arrows; the bull's-eye is the organization!

Figures 2-2 to 2-8 are guides to improving your resume and cover letter.

Once you have the virtual look nailed down, you can turn your attention to the physical you that you will present at the interview (assuming it is a face-to-face or televised meeting).

Your Physical Presence

Look Like You Work There Already

Are they a casual Friday outfit or casual 24/7? Are they suit and tie, Brooks Brothers, and conservative dressers? Do a little research, and you might find photos of management and/or employees in annual reports, on the company Web site or in newspaper articles. Given time, you could even scout the office and see what attire employees favor. Because time is an essential factor in

Types of Resumes

Chronological:

+ Highlights strong work history

+ Popular with traditional employers

− Can reveal gaps in work history

− Employer has to search for related skills/experience

Functional:

+ Focus on current skills, not prior jobs

+ Customer driven

+ Useful for those with spotty or diverse work histories

− Can be too narrow in approach

− Might not reveal clear job path

Combination Chronological-Functional:

+ Highlight skills not apparent in job history

+ Stresses experience related to job opening

− Could underemphasize work history

− Current goals not explained by work history

Alternative formats:

+ Innovative to support creativity element

+ Normal to include photo, graphics

− Can look like gimmick, amateurish

− Turn-off to conservative employers

Electronic (Internet):

+ Fast, inexpensive

+ Reach wide audience

− Uncertain of readership

− Use of key words can limit

Figure 2-2

Chronological Resume

Name
Address
City, State Zip
Phone/Fax/E-mail

Objective: Specific job/position

Summary: Candidate's qualifications targeted to job/organization

Professional
Experience:

Date:
(from-to)   Organization Name   City, State
Most recent Title/Position
              Description of responsibilities
                 Highlight key accomplishments

Date:
(from-to)   Organization Name   City, State
Next recent Title/Position
              Description of responsibilities
                 Highlight key accomplishments

Date:
(from-to)   Organization Name   City, State
Next recent Title/Position
              Description of responsibilities
                 Highlight key accomplishments

Education/
Professional
Training: Educational organization   City, State
              Degree received
              Seminars/workshops attended   City, State

Professional
Awards: Citations, awards

Affiliations: Professional associations, activities

Figure 2-3

Functional Resume

Name
Address
City, State Zip
Phone/Fax/E-mail

Objective: Specific job/position
Support with qualified accomplishments, proficiencies

Competency:
Priority Skill #1   Descriptive statement of transferable/ learned skills obtained through work experience
Accomplishments, qualified when possible

Competency:
Priority Skill #2   Descriptive statement of transferable/ learned skills obtained through work experience
Accomplishments, qualified when possible

Competency:
Priority Skill #3   Descriptive statement of transferable/ learned skills obtained through work experience
Accomplishments, qualified when possible

**Additional
Proficiencies:**   Related to job goal

**Employment
History:**

Organization	Title	City, State
Organization	Title	City, State
Organization	Title	City, State

**Education/
Professional
Training:**   Educational organization   City, State
Degree received
Seminars/workshops attended   City, State

**Professional
Awards:**   Citations, awards

Affiliations: Professional associations, activities

Figure 2-4

25

Online Resume

Name
Address
City, State Zip
Phone/Fax/E-mail

Keywords:
(list all the words associated with the job opening, your skills, experience, educational levels, and any technical expertise)

Objective:
Targeted to specific job or profession

Skills:
All the related soft and hard skills required for the job that you can offer

Experience:

Organization	City, State	From-to
Qualified details of responsibilities and skills used		

Organization	City, State	From-to
Qualified details of responsibilities and skills used		

Organization	City, State	From-to
Qualified details of responsibilities and skills used		

Education:

School	City, State	Degree earned

Seminars, workshops:

Achievements:

Figure 2-5

Resume Checklist

The main ideas:

✓ Targeted to job and organization

✓ Concise objective or summary

✓ Key selling points highlighted

✓ Information correct

✓ Experience qualified; numbers used when possible

✓ Format suited to experience level and job

✓ Includes contact information

✓ Excludes personal information (gender, race, age)

✓ Excludes salary history or requirements

✓ Consistent with cover letter

✓ "Voice" consistent with "actual" you

Visual presentation:

✓ Correct spelling

✓ Proper grammar

✓ Consistent tenses

✓ "Active" verbs used for traditional resumes

✓ "Keywords" used for electronic resumes

✓ Buzzwords or jargon eliminated

✓ 1 page; 2 for extensive experience sections

✓ Layout is crisp; well-proportioned margins, use of white space to separate sections

✓ Common section headings used

✓ Clean typeface: businesslike, uncluttered

✓ Quality printing: no smudges, good paper

Figure 2-6

Cover (Marketing) Letter Checklist

The Main Ideas:

✓ Addressed properly: correct name, title, address

✓ Targeted to specific job and organization

✓ First paragraph introduces you and the purpose of the letter

✓ Second paragraph is sales pitch; why they should hire you/invite you in for interview

✓ Strong closing indicates action you will take next

Visual:

✓ Paper coordinates with resume

✓ Letterhead is businesslike, correct contact information

✓ Correct spelling

✓ Proper grammar

✓ Consistent tenses

✓ Layout is crisp; well-proportioned margins

✓ Text not verbatim from resume; new or additional information that expands on or supports resume

✓ Use bullets, bolding, and underlining wisely to make letter reader friendly

✓ Signature

✓ Envelope professionally addressed; laser printed, typed or neatly handwritten

✓ Resume enclosed

✓ "Voice" consistent with resume

Figure 2-7

Cover or Marketing Letter

Name
Address
City, State Zip
Phone/Fax/E-mail

Name, Title
Department
Organization
Address
City, State Zip

Dear Mr./Ms./Mrs./Dr. _____

Spending last Tuesday with you interviewing for the position of —— was definitely the highlight of my week. Your enthusiasm for both the industry and for working at —— made an indelible impression on me. I was particularly impressed with the extensive tour of your operations department; it certainly is the heartbeat of the company.

As we discussed, my experience with —— and —— appear to particularly qualify me for the position, and the classes that I am currently enrolled in at —— will further prepare me to advance the technological support needed.

Your time and consideration is greatly appreciated. I do understand that you have just begun to search for candidates and would like to fill the position by year end. If there are any additional questions you need answered, please contact me. I will telephone you in approximately three weeks to follow up on the process.

Sincerely,

Signature

Figure 2-8

your preparation, you cannot go wrong in dressing in a classic out-fit: dress *UP* not *DOWN!* Dress for the job that you want (not nec-essarily for the job you have).

Note: if you are doing interviews on your lunch or before/after work, you might raise suspicions by being overly well dressed, so consider alternatives to wearing your "interview" outfits to work. Stop home and change, if possible, or use accessories such as a tie, scarf, and jacket/sport coat once you are out of the office to "dress up" or alter your appearance.

One interview question that is related to the whole clothing issue is *"Where does your manager/supervisor think that you are right now?"* Sneaking out of work or lying about "doctor's" appoint-ments' will not be impressive responses in an interview; stating that you asked for personal time/vacation time to attend to per-sonal business is both an acceptable and truthful response. This approach can explain why you might be dressed more for "work" than for an interview if you changed your schedule for a morn-ing or afternoon appointment, having no time to change outfits. If there is no opportunity to change, when scheduling your meeting, be sure to mention that you will not be able to be dressed as you would wish. You hope that they understand. When you state this you achieve two results. First, you put them on notice so that if there is any disappointment in your appearance, they were already aware that they might be. Second, you are dis-playing your serious intent and planned approach before the interview even starts.

As in many areas of the job search, common sense plays an important role in devising rules for personal appearance. Let's look at some key areas dealing with our physical look.

Grooming

- Neatly styled hair.
- Clean hands and nails, of reasonable length.
- Men: shaved or facial hair well groomed. Women: subtle makeup and hairstyles.
- No strong perfumes or aftershaves.
- Fresh breath and bright smile! They do not need to know what you ate for your last meal.

Attire

- Clean, pressed clothing at all times.

- Shoes in good repair and polished.

- Clothing should *not* make more of a statement than you do. Comfort is preferred to style or trendiness. A familiar outfit will be more comfortable to one you are wearing for the first time; this is not the time to tug, fidget, or be concerned about your clothing when you sit, stand, or walk. Take off those dry cleaning tags!

- Efficient bag or portfolio to carry extra copies of resume, last-minute notes to review, travel directions, and notepad. (See Chapter 3, What to Bring.)

- Most Americans favor the color blue; blue signals trust, confidence, and a sense of composure. (Other cultures and nationalities might have different colors associated with these traits.)

- Wear the brand—not the competition's! If interviewing at Armani, do not wear Tommy Hilfiger. If interviewing at *The New York Times*, do not come in carrying the *Daily News* under your arm.

- Real jewelry or understated jewelry. Leave the cloth watchbands, funny tie tacks, rhinestones, and novelty necklaces at home.

- Seasonal outerwear such as a winter or raincoat might be the first item the interviewer sees (*"May I take your coat?"*). Do not leave yourself open for embarrassment with overstuffed/torn pockets, ripped lining or loose/missing buttons. The same goes for your umbrella if you have one with you; make certain it can close properly, and do not leave it dripping on the company carpet.

- Leave the political/religious buttons at home—unless you do not mind the possibility of triggering a negative response from the interviewer.

Choose your outfit ahead of time, try it on, and look at yourself—front and back. Sit down in a low chair or couch. Walk up/down stairs. Make sure it works in all situations.

Telephone Interviews

Most often, telephone interviews are used as screening interviews for the employer to decide if they should invite you in for a face-to-face interview. It saves time and expense for the interviewer. Except for the obvious fact that the interviewer cannot see what you are wearing, the guidelines we have covered are still applicable. Some interviewers seem to prefer telephone interviews because they feel they are overly influenced by an applicant's appearance! Do not be tempted to wear ragged clothing or pajamas while being interviewed (even though you can); dressing professionally will make you feel professional on the telephone. Remember also that a smile conveys confidence in the tone of your voice. Also try standing when the interview takes place to give more energy to your voice.

Beyond telephones, there is also a growing use of televised interviews through videoconferencing or Web cams on the Internet. In those cases, physical appearance from the neck up can overshadow what you have to say; again, be conservative. Let the interviewer concentrate on what your verbal message is. You do not want to appear as a "floating head" if you wear dark clothing and are put against a dark background; aim for wearing contrasting colors. Deep blues with a pastel that complements your coloring can work for men and women. Take a cue from those television newscasters—go for elegant understatement! (See Figure 2-9.)

Head Games

Nonverbal communication is one area that is most neglected in a job applicant's preparation. Attaining the proper mind-set will send forth the needed facial expressions, body language, and "vibes" in the interview. These are most important in avoiding the "deer in the headlights" look, the "I pasted this smile on when I left the house" look, or the seemingly popular "poker face" in your interview.

This interview is a conversation, an exchange of ideas and information. Conversation should be engaged in; you must establish rapport with the interviewer. You want him/her to feel confident in your ability to do the job...so confident that the job is offered to you! You want to radiate confidence, professionalism and, above all, that you enjoy the process.

Telephone Tips

- Take telephone interviews seriously and prepare accordingly.
- Smile before you start! Create a friendly, open atmosphere.
- Note your accomplishment/achievement stories in advance to use in response to questions. Index cards are ideal formats.
- Prepare a fact sheet of your prior employers, specific dates; it is an expanded, detailed version of the resume you sent.
- List the five major points that you MUST make in the interview.
- Chose a time and place for the telephone interview that is quiet and private; turn off "call waiting" and any other telephones that may ring. A cell phone (unless it is excellent) is not recommended.
- Use a large table to organize and spread out your materials and notes; do not have paper shuffling noises as part of the conversation.
- Standing while talking will help you to maintain energy as well as focus.
- Modulate your tones and voice. Speak clearly.
- Do not interrupt or race through your responses. Pace yourself.
- If uncertain if you have answered a question completely, ask "Do you want further information?" You do not have visual clues to assess your responses.
- Allow interviewer to end the interview.
- Thank the interviewer at the end of the conversation and ask *"What is the next step?"*

Videoconferencing Tips

- Prepare and bring note cards or post-it notes that cannot be seen on camera.
- Arrive early at the site to determine setup and get comfortable.
- Arrange your notes so that you do not have to shuffle through them.
- Sit so that you are eye level with the camera.
- Check your posture. Don't fidget or gesture too much off camera.
- Smile...and enjoy the experience.

Figure 2-9

33

Relax

In the following chapters, you will research and rehearse for the interview. Do not forget the relaxation step! If you are given to anxiety, worry, or sleeplessness regarding interviews, remember that there are only two types of factors in any interview—those that you can control and those that you cannot. Doing the research and preparation for the interview pretty much takes care of the factors that you can control, so you do not need to worry about them. The rest—what will the interview be like, what questions will be raised, what biases might be present, will the interviewer be in a good mood, is there really a job opening—are totally outside of your control, so let them go. (See Figure 2-10.)

Eat healthy, get some exercise and fresh air, get a good night's sleep, check off your "To Do" list (see Chapter 12, Ten Crucial Last-

---

Interview Stress Reducers

Get a good night's sleep the night before.
Eat healthy.
Know that you are prepared.

- You know and understand the topic = YOU!
- You are motivated; you want this position, and you know why you want it.

Before you go into the interview, take a deep breath. Smile. Let the adrenalin flow. Get a little excited for the process itself.

Still shaky? Focus on your breathing...steady, deep.

Need more? Go into a quiet area or restroom and push hard on the wall. Transfer the stress; it will let the tension flow out of you.

Figure 2-10

Minute Checks), and enjoy your interview. Be confident that you have done your best to prepare and are an excellent—no, the best—candidate for the job. If you do not believe this, why should the interviewer? (See Figure 2-11.)

Last-Minute Checklist

☐ You have chosen a comfortable, suitable outfit to wear; it is clean, pressed, and ready.

☐ You have reviewed and printed extra copies of your resume.

☐ You have a copy of the "want" ad or job description.

☐ You have a copy of your marketing letter.

☐ You are excited but not stressed.

☐ You are confident that you can make a good presentation.

Figure 2-11

CHAPTER THREE

What to Bring

In Chapter 2, we attended to your virtual and physical selves. This chapter focuses on the three key items you need to bring with you on your interview:

- **What is in your head:** information and details regarding your past experience, skills, interests, and goals sufficient to generate targeted answers and to tell stories to illustrate them.
- **What is in your heart:** passion, enthusiasm, focus, drive, and all the reasons that are taking you to this interview.
- **What is in your hands**: pen and paper, some notes and information needed to complete an application if asked to do so, and a few more necessary items.

Bring the Knowledge of Your Past

When you prepared your resume, you might also have prepared a list of references, details of past jobs, and any achievements. This might be on a computer file or on little scraps of paper in a manila envelope. This dossier is not merely a trip down memory lane; the details can be extremely important if you are asked to complete a formal job application while at the interview site, and these details are even more essential in preparing for the questions you will be asked in an interview.

Regardless of how and where you have collected this information, it should be expanded, reviewed, and reorganized to jog your memory and seal up some "iffy" details. This information is a permanent part of your professional history and should continually be updated.

Become an Expert on You

"Tell me about a time when you..."
    "How would you deal with...?"
    "What is your experience with...?"

These are all types of questions raised in interviews, and there are no books, no Web sites that can help you answer them because the only one with the information to form the appropriate answer is you!

Certain aspects of your current/prior employment history are of interest to future employers; your ability to incorporate stories of achievements, projects, and responsibilities into your interview will "color" your responses and illustrate your current level of expertise. It is one thing to say, "Yes, I can take initiative" but more effective to be able to say "One time, at _____ I was faced with the problem of _____, which would seriously affect production. I took the initiative and _____, which resulted in _____."

Being able to relate a real-life example, to tell why it was important, what action you took, and what the outcome was will enable you to stand out from the other candidates and be the one the interviewer remembers because of the specific examples you gave.

To be able to not only come up with these illustrations and examples for your interview, but to match your skills to the skills required for the job, you have to bring all this information with you, in your head! This preparation is basic to the entire job search and interview process. You must be an expert on you— what you have done, how and why you did it, and what you can do next in this job and for this organization when hired.

Even though interviewers might seem to dwell on questions about your past, they are really more interested in what you can do now for their organization. Your ability to "roll forward" with your skills and experience—to elaborate on specifics from your past that are useful and valuable for them right now—will be prized in the interview. To do this, however, you must have a strong sense of what comprises your past experiences and how they relate to the job and organization that you want to turn into your next employer.

Details, Details, Details

Whether you generate your employment history by hand on a legal pad, in an Excel spreadsheet, or on index cards, it is more than a mere record-keeping exercise. Starting with your most current employer, provide as much of the information as possible using the format shown in Figure 3-1. (You will refer to this information in Chapter 10 when you prepare your answers to those questions most likely to be asked.) The more current the employer, the more information you should have available.

As you can see by the details requested, this can also be an outline for the preparation of a targeted resume, a cover letter, and/or an interview! Behavioral questions are questions that ask specifically for examples of your past performance (*i.e., "Tell me about a time when you..."*), and they need specific details for a great

Employment History

- Employer:
- Location/Address:
- Telephone #:
- Dates of Employment: from   to
- Starting Salary:
- Ending/Current Salary:
- Job Title:
- Corporate Title:
- Business of Organization:
- Department/Unit:
- Size of Organization:
- Size of Department:
- Gross Revenue/Profits:
- Name of Supervisor:
- Title of Supervisor:
- Names of Key Co-Workers/Peers:
- List Prime Responsibilities:
- List Achievements (What did you create, implement, design?)
- How did you affect income, costs, revenue?
- List Special Projects?
- List Skills Needed to Perform Job:
- List Skills Learned on the Job:
- Why Did You Take This Job?
- What Was Your Entry Position?
- What Was Your Initial Title?
- What Changes Did You Make to the Department?
- List Promotions/Commendations:
- Why Do You Want to Leave This Job?
- What Parts of the Job Do/Did You Like the Most?
- What Parts of the Job Do/Did You Like the Least?
- What Will Your Supervisor Say About Your Performance?

Figure 3-1

response. When asked *"What would your last supervisor say was your greatest contribution to the department?"* where do you think you will get the answer? Will you have your last supervisor's name even in mind, not to mention her opinion of you as well as her title?

There is no way you can practice a response ahead of time to every possible question you will be asked, but you certainly can have enough details, memories, and concepts in mind to generate intelligent responses about *yourself.* You should be able to let the interviewer know what facts in your history are relevant. For example, if you worked for an organization that had offices overseas and you were involved in handling foreign shipping procedures, the interviewer might not know that your former employer had global business activities. You might not have zeroed in on that piece of information if you had not gone through your work history in depth.

As you repeat the above format for former jobs, the less related they are to the job/organization you are setting your sights on or the further away in time, the less details you need to produce. You do need to relate prior jobs and experiences to the current job opening to show a link when applicable.

The Inner You

It might be a cliché, but you do wear your heart on your sleeve in every interview. Use this to your advantage! And make sure you bring the following important parts of yourself to your interview:

- **Your passion.** You are presenting yourself as a candidate that is enthusiastic about the job, about the organization, about the industry...even about the interview process itself! This is not the time for a *"been there, done that"* attitude. Whether you have been on 10 or 110 interviews already (or this really is your first one), you need to have a fresh and open mind. This is the first time you have interviewed with *this person* at *this company* for *this particular job.* It is a one-time shot. There are few opportunities for "do-overs" on botched interviews.

- **Use the anxiety that you might be feeling to boost your adrenalin.** You should be excited; a little nervousness is good. Arrogance and overconfidence breed sloppiness and can be easily detected. Having prepared brings your confidence level up a notch. Remind yourself of why you are a great candidate and why this is a mutually beneficial opportunity for you and the organization. (See Chapter 10 for preparing for the interview questions).

- **Be serious.** Imagine that you are being asked to make a presentation for a $250,000 or $1,000,000 deal. How careful would you be to get your facts straight, have a great sales pitch, and be confident in your presentation? Well, how much do you think this job is worth to you?

Practical Necessities

Granted, you are the most important item for the interview—the total virtual, physical, and historical you—but there are practical considerations also. Make sure you have all of the following:

- **Transportation**: How will you get to the interview? Do you have directions? Can you check ahead to make sure there are no construction delays? Do you know how long it will take to get there? Are there tolls to pay? If taking public transportation, do you know the route and stops? Plan your route carefully; when possible, check your directions with the company.

- **Your checklist of questions**: Do you have a list of questions *you* need answered? Gaps in information? What do you want to learn in the interview? (See Chapter 8 for help in preparing your list.) You will not whip the list out midinterview, but it will be part of your last-minute checklist; you can record the information garnered in the interview when you leave, while it is fresh in your mind.

- **Employment History**: In case you are asked to complete an application, you will need dates, addresses, phone numbers.

- **Education History**: If you are a recent (within the past five years) college graduate, review information about your school (name, address, phone number) and any courses that relate specifically to the job.

- **References:** If you are not presently employed, you might want to furnish a list of references for them to contact if asked to do so. Sometimes this information is requested on the application form as well. Should you not wish them to contact your current employer, they certainly will understand this, and you can furnish a list of prior employers with the understanding that if a firm job offer is made, you will be glad to provide contact information for your current employer at that time.

Everything else you need to bring should fit in your portfolio or bag. Please do not bring a suitcase! *Businesslike, confident,* and *efficient* are the key words for your appearance and demeanor. Travel light. (See Figure 3-2.)

Interview Necessities

1. Photo Identification Card; Proof of citizenship
2. Recent copies of resume
3. Business cards
4. Small tablet of paper
5. A professional-looking pen
6. Map or directions to interview site
7. Name and title of interviewer; correct spelling and pronunciation
8. Exact address of interview site; cross streets, floor, room number
9. Telephone # of interviewer
10. Your research notes on organization, industry, job
11. Your list of five main points you need to make
12. List of your questions to ask, information needed
13. List of references
14. Detailed employment history
15. Educational history
16. Work samples or portfolio if appropriate
17. Cell phone or pager turned off for meeting
18. Enthusiasm and confidence

Figure 3-2

The most important part of what you bring to the interview is you—not the clothes you wear but the skills and experiences that can turn you into a solution for the organization that hires you. (See Figure 3-3.)

Last-Minute Checklist

Interviews are easy if...

You are prepared.

☐ Know your strengths and weaknesses.

☐ Know the organization.

☐ Understand the job requirements.

☐ Match up your skills to their needs.

You face your worst fears in advance.

☐ What is the worst thing that can happen to you in the interview? (*They think I am too old/young/inexperienced/overqualified.*)

☐ What would be the worst possible outcome? (*I won't get this job. I might have to take a lesser paying job/less prestigious job/stay in my current job.*)

☐ Think opportunity! (*Too old? I have lots of contacts to boost sales. Too young? I have energy to spare and am a fast learner.*)

You sell yourself.

☐ Know why you are a good candidate and tell them.

☐ Show the value you will add.

You enjoy yourself.

☐ Radiate confidence in yourself; the interviewer will feel it too.

☐ You know all about yourself and are excited to tell your story.

☐ You are ready to listen, to really hear what you need to know.

Figure 3-3

CHAPTER FOUR

Interview Etiquette

It is not surprising that so many interviewers cite "poor manners" as a reason for turning down job applicants. Etiquette, or good manners, is defined as "customary rules for behavior in society." Well that certainly explains it!

Rules have been broken left and right in all areas of society, from casual Friday to "anything goes" every day. Headlines cite behavior on the part of key business executives that few could imagine years ago. Companies that have set the standards for products and professionalism have found themselves foundering, forcing huge layoffs and even closing their doors.

"Customs" change widely from one part of the country to another, from one sector of the business world to another. Some companies are returning to the conservative dress favored years ago, while others seemingly have thrown their collective hands in the air and said "whatever." It might be hard to tell what "customary" rules are anymore, but some basics can still be considered the standard.

Most of us appreciate having our name remembered once introduced and having it pronounced correctly. And being kept waiting for an appointment annoys many people. Not having someone look you in the eye while talking to you sets off bad vibes. The inability to share the floor during a conversation sets a poor tone. Being interrupted, being treated with prejudice of any kind, and being ignored do not make any of us feel good about the experience or the persons involved. Consider that the organization is seeking to attract good employees—such as yourself. Should not their manners and consideration reflect that attitude? You certainly will do your best to be a well-mannered, considerate interviewee.

Because the purpose of a job interview is to share ideas, it is important to quickly establish rapport between the interviewer(s) and the job candidate. Yet the very opposite happens in many interviews. The interviewer cannot get past some problems that hinder establishing rapport, not to mention not getting the job offer. What do interviewers cite as major interview faux pas? (See Figure 4-1.)

The sad thing is that almost all of these "errors" are avoidable (with the exception of getting caught in a sudden traffic accident or a mass transit delay, which can happen to anyone, despite planning ahead and leaving early). Obviously, some applicants are either so rattled when they go in for their interview that good manners go out the window, or they never knew the correct behavior in the first place. Most of etiquette is common sense— treating others with respect and

Common Interview Mistakes

- Arriving late
- Mispronouncing or not remembering the correct name of company/organization or the interviewer
- Smoking or smelling like an ashtray; chewing gum
- Talking too much
- Not talking enough
- The "zombie" effect a/k/a "deer in the headlights" look
- Bad-mouthing former employers
- Poorly or inappropriately dressed
- Poor hygiene
- Poor posture, slouching, fidgeting.
- Inability to make eye contact
- Too firm or limp handshake; not shaking hands
- Fidgeting, twitching, rubbing face, hair twirling
- Jangling or ostentatious jewelry
- "Know-it-all" attitude; name-dropping, jargon
- A "too humble" I-will-not-be-hired attitude

Figure 4-1

courtesy. Allowing for some cultural differences (some cultures might not consider shaking hands, for example, to be appropriate), most interviews adhere to some simple formats or unwritten rules.

Interview Rules

Even before the interview starts officially, you are being evaluated by every person that you meet at the organization. People in the elevator might be future coworkers. The receptionist might be the one who talks to everyone. Start off correctly—being polite, friendly, and courteous to all. (Keep your ears open: You should also be evaluating everyone to determine if this is a place where *you* want to work!) While waiting, do not slouch or sprawl in the reception area. If needed, ask for a restroom to freshen your hair or makeup. Smile warmly and confidently. Please do not have long, extended cell phone conversations that all can hear. In fact, you should be sure to turn off your cell phone until you leave the building.

Greetings—The Interview is Officially Started

Finally, you hear your name called. You stand, shake hands, and introduce yourself, using the other person's name (pronounced correctly). The interviewer should initiate the introduction and handshake, and you should respond:

> Hello. I am Joe Blanks. Mr. Evans, I am so pleased that you are able to take the time this afternoon to meet with me to discuss the engineering position.

You have confirmed who you are (and how to pronounce your name as well as the fact you like to be called "Joe," not "Joseph"), why you are there and that you know whom you are meeting with! You have spoken in a clear voice, not mumbling or rushing out your words. You are already starting great!

Listening versus Hearing

There is a difference between *hearing* and *listening*. You can be hearing music while working on the computer, but are you *actively listening?*

- How many times have you been introduced to someone new and never "heard" his or her name because you were so intent on having your name said correctly?
- Ever have your mind wander during a business meeting, thinking about what was to be done that afternoon—and been surprised with being asked a question?
- Or, going over some details with friends or associates before an event, can you literally feel that they have "tuned out?"

We spend years in school learning to read and write but no time learning to listen. Active listening—participating in the conversation—requires skill and practice. It is worse because we all seem to think, *"I know how to do that."* Check out one of the talk shows or news programs (the ones where the guests and hosts are NOT yelling at each other). Turn off the sound and watch the body language, the facial expressions, the hand gestures; you can tell a lot about how the conversation is going by all these nonverbal details. The same is true in an interview. The combination of your verbal and nonverbal messages can reveal more than you wanted to!

How to Be an Active Listener

"Active" listening implies participation—a mutual sending and receiving of messages. It is just as important for you to be sensitive to the messages, both verbal and nonverbal, that the interviewer is sending as it is for you to monitor all the messages that you are sending. To ignore some of these signals or to misread them can prove to be more than bad manners; it could cost you the job offer. (See Figure 4-2.)

The Other Side of the Desk

It is also possible that the interviewer has left his/her manners outside the door. Worse yet, that person might never have learned how to behave professionally or give a good interview. Aside from wringing your hands and hoping the whole ordeal is over with quickly and painlessly, what can you do when faced with a problematic interviewer? (See Figure 4-3.)

Other Etiquette Issues

- **Keep it businesslike.** Regardless of the family photos, pictures of sailboats, or little statues of horses that decorate the interviewer's office, do not make personal comments. You might have the best of intentions but end up with the worst of reactions.

- **How do you pull yourself out of the hole you innocently dug for yourself by commenting on the interviewer's handsome son in the photo**—only to find out it is a daughter?

- **Trying to break the ice by sharing your love of horses too**—only to turn the entire interview into a chat about breeding stock and never talking about you or the job?

Active Listening Skills

- **Make eye contact.** Not staring...but do maintain focus on speaker.
- **Pay attention.** Do not think of your answer while the other person is talking. Concentrate on what the other person is saying.
- **Offer feedback.**

  <u>Verbally</u>, by saying *"Yes, I see."* or *"That is true."* or *"I never thought of that."* to show that you are following along.

  <u>Physically</u>, by eye contact, smiling encouragingly, nodding, facial expressions that show concurrence, understanding.
- **Slow it down.** Do not rush to answer every question. Stop to think when needed. It is perfectly alright to say, *"Let me think about that for a moment."*
- **Take turns.** Neither party should treat the interview like a monologue.
- **Do not assume anything.**
- **Use empathy.**

Figure 4-2

- **Compliment him/her on the great boat**—only to find it recently was seriously damaged.
- **Let the interviewer finish.** Do not be like the "losers" on the game shows that ring the buzzer too fast to blurt out the wrong answer because they did not hear the entire question. Let him/her finish talking. It is OK to pause from time to time to gather your thoughts, just do not make those "thinking" sounds *errrrr—ummmmm—hmmmmmm*). If you are not certain you understood the question, do not be afraid to ask: *"Were you asking me if I ever was responsible for hiring any of my staff or just involved in the process?"* Restating the question as a preface to your answer is one way to get a moment or two to form your response.

Problem Interviewers

Interviewer is:	*You can offset by:*
Unprepared	Offering copy of resume Allow him/her to come up to speed. *"I appreciate your seeing me for the position of _____. I was referred by _____."*
Distracted	Offer to reschedule interview for a better time. *"As I was just saying..."* to bring back to topic.
Argumentative	Don't rise to any bait. Remain friendly and professional. *"I really do not bring my politics into the office, but I can see the topic is of importance to you."*
Hidden Agenda	Try to bring back to purpose of interview. *"Is there something I can add to my answer?"* *"Will that provide you with the information you need?"*
Monologist	Turn it back into a conversation. Repeatedly, if needed. *"I appreciate you sharing your experiences with me. I was hoping that my experience with _____ would be what you were looking for."*
Uninvolved	Remind him/her of why you are there. *"We spoke on the telephone yesterday. I answered the ad for _____ and am currently working for _____ as a _____."*

Figure 4-3

- **Leave your emotions at the door.** You might be having a very bad day before you walk into the interview. Do not bring those negative energies into the meeting. Likewise, the interviewer might have heard some distressing news before you arrived, but it should not factor into the proceedings.

- **Maintain your own space.** Do not spread out in the chair or lean on the table or desk. Do not touch things on the desk or table.

- **Concentrate.** The best advice for being a successful listener is to be "in the moment." This means not to be tied up thinking of what you have to say next, what might be asked, or what the interviewer is thinking of your performance to date. If you are defensive or taking the process too personally, you cannot be listening. If you are not listening, you might be missing the salient points of the interview. (See Figure 4-4.)

Body Language Tips

- **Good posture** will keep you alert as well as looking professional and interested in the proceedings.
- Constantly **gesturing** can be distracting. Keep gestures to a minimum and use effectively when appropriate.
- **Do not lean** on desks, tables. Maintain your own space.
- **Do not fidget** with clothing, papers, hair, face, hands, nails.
- **Sit with legs straight** or ankles crossed. Do not cross your legs or sit sprawled.
- **Facial expressions** should be friendly and appropriate to the conversation. Your smile should not be pasted on. A tilted head shows interest.
- **Voice should be clear** and well spoken. Too loud or too soft a speaking tone sends their own messages.
- **Handshake** at greeting and exit should be firm and dry.
- **Crossing arms** across your chest can appear defensive or closed to communication.
- **Rolling eyes,** blinking, or looking downward sends negative messages.

Figure 4-4

Now that you know how to behave professionally and courteously in an interview, remember these guidelines to evaluate how your interviewer treats you; it might be the hallmark of how the organization treats its employees. (See Figure 4-5.)

Last-Minute Checklist

☐ Be on time. Be a few minutes early to allow you to make any last-minute adjustments or preparations.

Being late says you do not care.

Being too early says you are overanxious.

☐ Be confident. You can answer their questions.

☐ Be open and friendly to all you meet.

☐ Be able to repeat the names of all you are introduced to.

"It is a pleasure to meet you, Ms. _____."

☐ Be polite. Use their title : Mr. Mrs. Ms. Unless invited to use first names, then reciprocate.

☐ Be aware of your surroundings but do not spend time looking about or staring.

☐ Do not look at your watch or clock repeatedly.

☐ Respect your interviewer but do not be overawed by the "Giver of jobs" role they are in.

☐ Be aware of your body language.

☐ Be appreciative of the time and consideration given you.

Figure 4-5

Defining Your Winning Game Plan

CHAPTER FIVE

Researching the Company in Four Easy Steps

For every interview, you need to answer for yourself the following question: Why do I want to work for this organization? You might or might not be asked this question outright in the interview, but you certainly need to know all the pertinent facts for yourself before you sit down across a desk from an interviewer. (See Figure 5-1.)

There is a great telecom company headquartered in New Haven, Connecticut, that took as part of its name the suffix "dot.net." When they were experiencing a period of extremely high growth, it was appalling how many times their recruiters would ask, intended as a friendly, open-ended, ice-breaker question, *"What do you know about our company?"* and get for a reply, *"It is a dot-com, isn"t it?"* at a time when being a dot-com seemed a wave of the future. Obviously, those job candidates did *not* do their research ahead of time.

When it comes to doing your own research, start with yourself and have a very selfish motive for expressing any interest in any organization. You need to ask what makes this organization one where you want to spend more hours than anywhere else. Due diligence is more important than ever. There is certainly and should be an interest in avoiding organizations like preformed Enron and HealthSouth. (*Fortune* magazine described HealthSouth CEO Richard Scrushy in a recent article as one who would frequently make the statement *"That is the stupidest thing I ever heard,"* at his weekly Monday morning meetings with his senior staff. Would you want to work in that kind of environment? If you are not careful and neglect your homework, you will.) The saddest part is that by taking a job unknowingly at an organization that has major weaknesses (or one that just might not be the best fit for you), you will also be losing out in another way. With four simple research steps,

Why Do the Research?

1. So you can sound intelligent in the interview.
2. So that you can decide if this is an organization that you want to work for.

Figure 5-1

you might find an organization where your time and energies will be put to better use!

Don't waste time; use what you have to maximize your knowledge and preparation. (See Figure 5-2.)

People—Whom Do You Know?

The first channel to pursue is people. *Whom do you know?*

Make a list of any and all persons you know who work, have worked, or are about to start working for the organization you are scheduled to meet with; extend the list to anyone who works for a supplier, client, or even a competitor. Consider everybody —family, friends, neighbors, and acquaintances. Mark this list "direct access." These are the persons who you know have had a direct relationship with the organization now, in the past, or are about to, and they possess knowledge that will certainly be useful to you. Even if the person you consider turned down a job or was fired, that person might prove helpful. These are the people you should contact immediately for some insight into the organization or job. (Evaluate the information once you have it, but the primary goal of this exercise is to gather as much data as possible so you can then determine how that information will be useful to you.)

Once you have exhausted temporarily (maybe more will come later) all of your direct access contacts, then move on to the second layer to identify those who might know someone who is currently working, has worked, or is about to work there. For the third layer, look for those who either are customers, suppliers, vendors, or any-

---

The Four Steps

- People: whom do you know?
- Electronic research
- Print media; libraries
- Organization's publications

Figure 5-2

one who, in whatever capacity, has had contact with the organization for whatever reason or knows someone who is a customer; include those who have decided not to be customers. (See Figure 5-3.)

This is an opportunity for you—if you have the time—to interview someone else for information you need. If using the phone is the only way, due to the limited time you have, it will certainly do. The key is to gather as much data as you can before the meeting so you will know as much as you can.

Electronic Research

A second major source of information that will allow you to perform the research you need is the electronic marketplace. There is more data to mine than ever before due to the proliferation of the world's greatest information distribution system, the Internet. You need to perform electronic research by surfing the Web to discover

---

Open-Ended Questions to Ask

- How long were you associated with organization _____?
- In what capacity?
- What do/did you like about organization _____?
- What has been your experience with them?
- What do you feel are their strong points?
- What do you feel are their weak areas?
- What do you know about (job/position)?

If the person has knowledge of you and your work experience:
- Do you think I would be successful in this organization?
- What do you think my biggest problem would be?
- What advice could you give me for my interview with _____?

Figure 5-3

relevant Web sites, and utilize effective search engines. Your approach must be *"I know the information is there, but how am I going to find it? Where should I look?"*

The place to start this second research step is at the organization's Web site. Either get there directly by taking the organization's name and tagging on the suffix ".com" or ".biz" or ".org," or try doing a search on a Web-based search engine. If you do not gain access when you try to go directly to the organization's Web site, waste no time. Go to a search engine such as Google or AlltheWeb or Yahoo. If you have access to a Bloomberg terminal, go there for information as well, but don't waste time if you don't already know how to use it. The benefit of using a search engine is that you will not only get the URL needed to access the Web site, but you will also be provided with citations for all recent mentions in business, trade, and general-interest periodicals, as well as articles written by staff writers on the periodical's payroll and not the organization's.

When conducting online research, always check out the organization's Web site. First, critique its look. Is it bland, stodgy, edgy, or something in between? Explore it to get to know everything the organization wishes to share with all visitors to its Web site. Then look for its annual report and a list of recent articles that have appeared in the press. Check out the career portion of the Web site to see if the position you are interviewing for is posted. If it is, get the job description. Secondly, see what other positions are available and, if stated, how long that position has been online. Third, who is the person identified as the contact? Fourth, what do they say about their benefits? This is all quick, useful preparation for getting ready for your interview that—with access to the Internet— takes very little time.

At the Google Web site, you should also search for information regarding the person(s) you are to meet with. Google frequently will provide information, on an ongoing basis, that will alert you to name mentions for all and any items of which it is aware. You might learn that the person you are meeting with is an alumnus of LMN University and ran the marathon last year. There might also be a news article that includes a picture that was published by a local newspaper covering a community event that the organization sponsored. In the interview, be certain, however, that you are not projecting the image of an electronic stalker or snooper. One enthusiastic applicant, in an effort to show how much he wanted to work for the organization, mentioned to his interviewer that he was impressed that she had been given an award during her graduate studies for a team-based project. He knew it was a mistake when the interviewer became visibly annoyed that he had learned this about her, and yet he would not relent and continued to boast that he had obtained the information on the Internet. (See Figure 5-4.)

Other Web sites are dumping grounds for disgruntled employees, central points of contact for "alumni," and still others are created by happy or displeased customers. *Vault.com* is one such Web site.

What information should you have at your fingertips, prior to each and every meeting with any organization that agrees to meet with you — whether the organization is considering you for a job, or has agreed to discuss job leads, or meet with you for an information session?

- **First, be sure you have the correct name and spelling of the organization (take nothing for granted!).** The correct name of one organization is The Mitsubishi Trust and Banking

---

Prime Search Engines

1. *http://www.google.com*
2. *http://www.alltheweb.com*
3. *http://www.yahoo.com*
4. *http://search.msn.com*
5. *http://aolsearch.aol.com* (internal)
   http://search.aol.com/(external)
6. *http://www.askjeeves.com*
7. *http://www.hotbot.com*
8. *http://www.lycos.com*
9. *http://www.teoma.com*

Information provided by *www.searchenginewatch.com*

Figure 5-4

Corporation. Leaving the "The" out of the title is considered a major affront and a clear sign that the offender has not done his/her homework. JPMorgan Chase is spelled without spaces and has caps where it wants them. If you are sending any letters there, be sure to do the same.

- **Determine the business the organization is in.** If you think all banks are the same, just look up the two mentioned above on the Internet to determine the variety of ways that one is distinguished from the other. An easy determinant is to consider the major source of revenue. What products/services does the organization sell, and what do they emphasize in their advertising materials? Do not assume that if you are interviewing at a "not for profit," government agency or hospital/health care agency that they are generic either. Know what they do and how they do it.

- **Next, determine how the specific unit in which your position and/or interviewer is located fits into the overall organization.** Is it a line or staff function? Line functions are those of primary value to the organization and directly aligned with the success of its "sales" efforts. For an auto company, a main driver is its auto sales. For another consumer-oriented company, such as beverages, it might be its market share. For a pharmaceutical company, it might be research and development. Staff functions are those that "support" the entire organization so that each of its members can do their jobs. Finance, Accounting, Payroll, Security, Facilities, Legal, and Human Resources are always included here. When the term "internal customers" is used, the function is a staff function.

- **Learn about the management and key leaders.** You also will want to know who is running the organization (the names of the leadership are usually prominently displayed on the organization's Web site. Try the "About us" link). Read any press releases for recent senior/key appointments (as well as ages). Seek out the most recent developments—earnings reports, promotions, mergers and acquisitions. Where did these leaders come from? Look too for the organization's most recent releases. If, for example, the organization's most recent press release is seven months old, either not too much has been happening lately or the Web site is not up to date. Are they cutting expenses? Web site maintenance is frequently one of the first areas to go.

Do not ignore industry Web sites. If the organization is in the paper industry, reading about the industry itself and perhaps discovering the organization's standing in that industry will provide another level of insight.

If there is time, a wealth of information can also be discovered by a visit to either one of the organization's retail sites or corporate offices.

Print Media

The third channel to pursue includes industry newspapers, as well as general interest and trade magazines and periodical guides. For whatever reason, your Web-based search might not identify all the articles where the organization and/or its senior members of management are mentioned in the press. You will only have found the ones included in the search engines as part of their sweep when you performed your electronic searches. Frequently, differences in names and references to organizational titles might miss important articles, so you need to be sure during the conducting of your research to use the more traditional—and still complete— approach. Alternatively, you might not have access to the Internet to do the online research.

If there is time, the best one-stop source for information is the local branch of the public library. In spite of all the budget constraints and pronouncements of the Internet gurus, the local library continues to have a long-standing reputation for the best single source for recent articles by subject. One of the reasons for that reputation is that it always has a complete copy of the *Readers Guide to Periodical Literature.* The other great reason for the library as a great reference source that continues to be underrated is the local librarian. Librarians continue, for whatever reason, to be ignored professionally in spite of the fact that they are uniquely positioned to be knowledge gatekeepers in this electronic and information age. They are disciplined and thoroughly trained, with a passion, as well as a respect, for information that is unsurpassed.

The Organization's Own Publications

The fourth and last channel to go to, in an effort to ensure that your research has been thorough and complete, is to the organizations own publications—including, but not limited to, its most recent annual report and 10K. Thanks to the current perceived need for all organizations to insist on putting as much as possible on a company Web site, it is easier than ever to obtain the most recent annual report and 10K. Again thanks to the Internet and most organizations belief that they need to have a presence on it, the organizations Web site is also the place to go for most recent quarterly reports and up-to date press releases. Include a review of these before your interview to ensure that you are as up to the minute as you can be on any current changes in the marketplace and challenges the organization faces. Two reasons for this—first to strengthen or detract from the reasons you had been considering the organization and second to show your potential employer that you are as current and up-to-date as they are. (Once in a while, you will even find that the information that you obtained from their own Web site is news to them!)

What to Look for When Going through the Organization's Material

Consider both the form and content of what you are reviewing. (See Figure 5-5.)

- What is the "look" of the organization's communications pieces? Traditional? Contemporary? State-of-the-art/edgy?
- Does it fit with the business they are in?
- What does the letter from the chairman/CEO say?

Look for inconsistencies: Does it boast that employees are their most valued assets, but they just had major layoffs? Do they address both issues, or do they speak in one voice and act in another? The better organizations will be consistent in their messages. Look at the pictures they chose to include. Do they include other members of management? Is the team diverse? Young or old? Are employees, customers included? What about revenue—how much did they sell? Is it more or less than the years before? Is the reason

It Is Good to Know...

Organizational history
Organization structure
Officers; biographical sketches/information
Number of employees
Products and services
Financial information: sales, profitability, and efficiency
Recent developments: products, services, and facilities
Number of hours in an average working day; shifts
Work ethic
Perks
Hiring process
Diversity

What about the industry ?

Current environment
Trends
Industry norms and key ratios
Market share
Forecasts
Major players

Figure 5-5

for increased sales due to special circumstances—a major merger or acquisition? What were the primary products/services? Are they making money? Have they been consistently? Does it look like they will continue to do so in the future? (Does the Chairman's letter warn of more difficult times ahead?)

Take a look at the pay information provided in their 10(K) report—what did the highest five executives get paid last year? Is that high, low, or average for that industry? What is their financial condition? Go to the back of the annual report. What functions do the officials of the organization take responsibility for? The CEO, COO, and CFO will always be listed, but what other functions are named? Is the area that you are meeting with mentioned? Do you know any of the names? In addition, is the head of the Human Resources function included? If not, what does this say about the organization and how important it considers the function and its people? After reviewing the materials, ask yourself what business the organization is in, and does this change your opinion of what you think the objective of the organization is? (See Figures 5-6 and 5-7.)

Research Web Sites

http://www.job-interview.net/ Industry and career information

http://www.wetfeet.com/ Organization/industry information

http://www.vault.com/companies Corporate information

http://www.hoovers.com/free/ Corporate information

http://www.zapdata.com Annual Reports

Also...the online versions of

- *Fortune*
- *Wall Street Journal*
- *Barrons*
- *The New York Times*
- *Newsweek*
- Your local newspapers
- Trade or industry publications

Figure 5-6

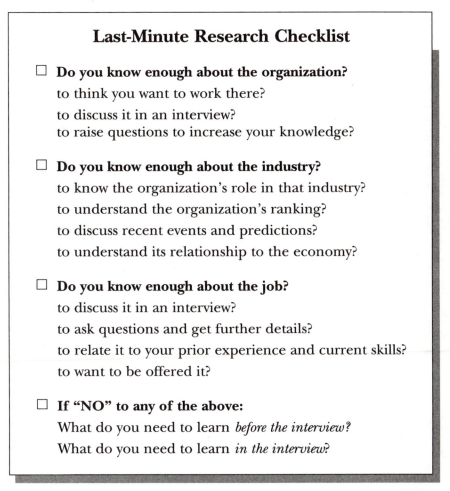

Last-Minute Research Checklist

☐ **Do you know enough about the organization?**
to think you want to work there?
to discuss it in an interview?
to raise questions to increase your knowledge?

☐ **Do you know enough about the industry?**
to know the organization's role in that industry?
to understand the organization's ranking?
to discuss recent events and predictions?
to understand its relationship to the economy?

☐ **Do you know enough about the job?**
to discuss it in an interview?
to ask questions and get further details?
to relate it to your prior experience and current skills?
to want to be offered it?

☐ **If "NO" to any of the above:**
What do you need to learn *before the interview*?
What do you need to learn *in the interview*?

Figure 5-7

CHAPTER SIX

Understanding Your Competition

For three reasons, you need to be mindful of various types of competition throughout the interview process and identify any signals of their increasing impact as quickly as they occur. First, you need to be sure that you don't take the perception of unidentified competitors personally because, as you will discover below, it is quite possible that causes affecting the delay of extending a job offer to you have nothing to do with you. Second, if you recognize your competition for what it is, you will then be able to determine what, if anything, you can do about it. Third, remember to strengthen your resolve to continue to press on with your job search, regardless of how "locked-in" any situation appears. Like a storm looming off shore—hesitancy and doubt on the part of your potential employer might suddenly appear at any time and radically change the conditions and opportunity that looked so positive and definite just days—or moments—before.

As you meet with the company within the next 24 hours, you might quickly realize that any of the categories shown in Figure 6-1 might be the specific competition you face head-on. So be ready for them.

Time and Indecision

Before you meet with any employer, realize with *what* and with *whom* you are competing. Unfortunately, it is not just about people. (See Figure 6-1.)

Employers: Your "Other" Competition

Unwillingness to make a decision now.

Deciding not to hire at all.

Position already filled.

Budget cuts; hiring freeze.

Inexperienced, disorganized, unfocused hiring manager(s).

Figure 6-1

In this softest of job markets, more frequently than not the recruitment and selection process is stretched out more than at any time in recent memory. The question that easily comes to mind is *"What are they thinking?"* If no one has been in the open position for a while, the company should really address the issue of whether the position should be filled at all. It seems in these instances the thinking is, *"We absolutely need to fill this position, but not just right now."* It boggles the mind because if the position needs to be filled, then:

1. What drives these otherwise decisive individuals to delay any decision to fill it?
2. Who is doing the work of the unoccupied position?
3. What message does the unfilled position send to those currently employed at that organization?

No Decision for Now

In the first scenario, the position is vacant and the necessary approvals are in place to fill it. Yet there is an unwillingness to fill the position (even though there might be a budget increase). It might be that there is a new manager who has just started and she is reevaluating the department's structure. It might be that a decision maker at that level or above is concerned about the change in business conditions (down or up) and is "placing the position on hold" at this time. Perhaps the supervisor is away (business trip, vacation, birth of a child, adoption of a child located in some distant land). They might be having second thoughts about going inside, or they might be concerned about the job description itself, or they just became aware that an ex-employee has surfaced. Alternatively, they might have decided, for whatever reason, not to fill the position.

Your strategy here should be to determine whether to devote more time and energy to pursuing them. Even if you have no intentions to, ask them when you are told about the decision they have made to wait, when (not if!) you should follow up. If nothing else, you are acting professionally while at the same time hiding your emotions and disappointment.

No Hire at All

Consider this unfortunate scenario that actually does happen. You have been through the process and met 12 people. The lengthy application has been completed and your references have been checked. After trying to place a phone call to the internal point person for four days, you finally hear that they have decided to pull the search and not fill the position at all. They appreciate your interest and if the position—or another suitable one surfaces—they promise to call. Best wishes in your job search.

It happens. Your first (or later) thoughts might turn to conspiracy theories with one or more of your suspect references in mind. Review the situation so that you are certain it was not anything your references said or didn't say (make sure you always let your references know before you give their names). More likely than not, your references were not the problem and the position was pulled just like the organization said. If you really liked the organization and would like to keep in touch, suggest that you would like to and then do so. Identify, from all with whom you met, the person who will be the key point of contact that would be the most effective communication link going forward. If you had some questions about the job or the organization, now is the time to review them and jot them down so that you can refer to these questions if the organization continues to pursue you again later.

Already Filled Position

What, you might ask, would the reason be for inviting you in for an interview if they already filled the position? This is a good question and one that you need them to answer before you leave the meeting. The best approach is to always get them to tell you without having to ask. Ask only as a last resort.

If you are effective in getting the interviewer to share the reason for the invitation, although the position has already been filled, the answer will be less guarded and more open. Be sure to listen very carefully to each and every word and watch the facial expressions throughout. Reasons might vary from the weakest ("We had already agreed to meet with you, so we thought it best not to cancel.")—to the strongest ("We really liked your resume and want to get you to join our organization. Even though you applied for _____ position, that spot had already been filled when you applied, but we do have an opening in the _____ department. Would you consider working for us there?")

There might also be other reasons, so be on the alert. If you worked for Martha Stewart or Donald Trump, you might have their aura on your persona, unbelievably, and if the interviewer happens to be a stargazer, s/he might want to meet with you to hear "what he was really like." Another reason might be that the interviewer has been asked to see you by his/her supervisor, who obviously was too embarrassed to cancel. The supervisor has someone else meet with you because the position was filled and she felt uncomfortable canceling your meeting.

Regardless of the reason given for making you come in to meet with her, even though the position is already filled, still try your best to hide your disappointment. Use the interview as a learning experience to sharpen your skills. More importantly, see if you can unearth other opportunities either inside or outside the organization. Remember that the interviewer is vulnerable and therefore will more probably be inclined to do something for you. Watch out for the really rude ones who will quickly mention to you that the position has been filled and they have very little time while they try to end the interview before it even begins. One last comment—always review the situation to be sure that you don't—unbeknownst to you—have a banana sticking out of your ear or some other faux pas. (Try to visit the restroom upon your five-minute early arrival to reduce the likelihood of that happening and give a boost to your confidence, knowing that you have checked yourself out and are therefore able to confirm that you do look sharp.)

Budget Cuts

Here the reason is more specific. Hear the interviewer out to determine how deep and how long the condition appears. Listen carefully to the cause(s) she offers. If she doesn't give specific reasons, be sure to ask—she does owe you some explanation for the imposition she has made on your time. Find out the reason she decided to meet with you if no job is in the offing—as with the other scenarios above, rather than just walk away from the meeting disgusted. Remember—it is not about you.

Look for opportunities to take the offensive. In this budget scenario, you have an opportunity to demonstrate your value-added skills that they cannot afford to be without because of the fiscal challenges they describe. When given the opening, mention quickly how you saved ABC Corporation XX dollars in direct costs and now you wonder if perhaps the same approach would apply here. If they cannot increase their head count, suggest that they take you on as a consultant on a per-diem rate. The key is to not be so disappointed that you just leave because the position you were so certain about just went up in smoke. You owe it to yourself to see whether there is an alternative opportunity there or elsewhere (does she know anyone who is also looking to fill a similar position?).

Skills and Talents (or Lack Thereof) of Those Who Are Involved in the Process

There might be some other bizarre things going on in an organization as it searches for talent that you need to be mindful of. Knowing these things can strengthen your resolve as you go through this job-searching process and help you continually remember that you should never take it personally when you get no callbacks and no decisions. Consider a couple of examples from a recent *New York Times* article on the careers page of the Sunday Classified Ads section. The article focused on two Human Resource professionals and the approaches they take to screen applicants. In the first example, the HR professional stated that she is too overwhelmed by all the resumes she receives in response to any ad that she runs, so her solution has been to hire a temp to screen resumes. She only considers the resumes of those persons who have been selected by the temp for additional consideration. The article doesn't describe the skill set of the temp. Even if the temp had significant HR and specific resume-screening experience, she lacks organizational knowledge—an important missing ingredient for one entrusted with such an important responsibility.

The second example is even more odd. There is an HR professional who feels she is so overwhelmed by resumes in response to the open positions in her organization that she shares with the reporter her secret to solving the problem. Are you ready? She tells the reporter from *The New York Times* that she only looks at every fifth one. Honest.

The point we are making here is that in addition to the candidates with whom you are contending for visibility, you need to consider the competency of the resume screeners. Realize that you might come up against a "take just one out of every fiver." (Congratulations, yours was the fifth resume and now you get to meet the person responsible for that approach.) You might even be screened by a temp who does not have a clue about the requirements needed for the open position.

A word of caution—regardless of the skill level, age, perceived competence, or any other factor that causes you to evaluate the interviewer's competency, do not let your guard down or do anything that will negate any opportunity you have for consideration. Always be professional. Hide any disappointment and keep trying to win the person over. Hillary Clinton allowed herself to once be interviewed by David Letterman's mother on his show. Hillary was so winning in her efforts to work with Dave's mom and make her look like *the* star. You need to do the same and never, ever consider doing anything that would eliminate any chance for further consideration when faced with incompetence or worse, disinterest.

All Those Other Applicants

When thinking about the other applicants with whom you might be competing, remember the three elements that employers consider when meeting with candidates. First, your invitation is based on the strength of your resume, and you have been selected for an interview because, from your resume, it appears that the job for which you are being considered is one that you have the ability to perform.

It gets more difficult to determine whether you have the other two requirements, though—motivation and fit. At your meeting, you have to be prepared to show that you have not only the willingness but also the passion to complete the job, and be alert to the fact that you will not get around those you annoy during the process.

Concentrate on your passionate side and then your congeniality, and you will win every time. Rest assured that your competition will be trying to do the same. Your goal is to convince your interviewer that your uniqueness is what distinguishes you from all the other applicants (inside and outside the organization), and the organization will truly be more effective if the interviewer is able to convince you to join them. (See Figure 6-2.)

In-House Applicants/Candidates

The decision to look inside before considering outside candidates is one every well-run organization makes. In theory, the decision

Your Obvious Competition

Other in-house applicants
All those outside applicants
Yourself

Figure 6-2

should be made and the recruitment and selection process remain internal before any efforts to "go outside." Job posting is frequently the method of choice to ferret out internal candidates. With the PC, even the remotest outposts of the most global organizations have access to job posting that is only delayed by time zone changes, so employees who wish to be considered candidates for open positions are certainly able to apply. Moreover, frankly with all due respect to you, the reader, that is as it should be. So you might be puzzled by the fact that we are discussing this at all. If open positions are first considered in light of internal candidates, it seems that these openings, if filled from within, would never see the light of day to the outside world. An organization has an opening. An internal candidate is found (perhaps a subordinate in the same department). Position filled. What happens in practice, though, makes this review a little more complicated (even in the most local, single location organizations). Let us explain.

Frequently potential internal candidates, for whatever reason, don't surface at the start of the search. Many times department heads will ask HR staff to jump-start the search to see what the market is like. In this weak job market, this approach is further clouded by the false perception that there is a ton of talent out there (that is much stronger than internal staff!) looking for work and willing to perform any job at a low rate of pay. In an effort to comply, HR then starts the search and identifies candidates, like you, who sooner or later are invited in. When they meet with you, even though they don't say so, they are determining whether your skill set and talents are stronger than any of their current employees. Assume this is so at every job search meeting you attend. You need to demonstrate the advantage they would have in hiring you with your outside expertise at every chance that you get at every one of those meetings. "Accentuate the positive," as the old song says. Avoid any mention of internal staff. If you do, you might be reminding them of something they had not considered and you have inadvertently created internal competition they might otherwise completely have ignored.

Outside Applicants

This is the toughest competition of all. When other outside applicants are your competition, you are in fact competing with the world for one job. How daunting is that? To further add to your concerns, the most qualified person will be less likely to get the job than the person who is best at interviewing. To add to your discomfort, be sure to remember that outside applicants also include ex-employees and referrals.

How can you deal with all these folks? The three "R's" are very useful to remember at this point. If you did your research and you rehearsed your interview, now you should be confident in your preparation so that you can relax and enjoy your meeting. Don't get too comfortable because you want to stay focused and not let your guard down at any time.

Yourself as Your Worst Competitor

It is a fact that there are many more applicants than positions available (even for great positions in the growth industries of health care and education). Accept it. Accept too the fact that in addition to the number of candidates you need to compete with to get a job offer, there are also other factors and extenuating circumstances that will impact your ability to turn all your efforts into a completed job search. Preparation and confidence are the two essential elements that you need to be ready for in any meetings you arrange. By taking care of what you can, you are as in control of your side as you can be. What happens from there is not totally your call or your fault. Once you give your best, the rest is up to them because it still remains a highly subjective decision on the employer's part.

Negative energy, despite your best efforts, can creep into an interview. It can start with the interviewer's comment that *"You are the perfect candidate, but unfortunately we have been asked to hire a referral."* Or even before the meeting, a receptionist can make you wait until he has completed dealing with other business. It might be caused by the simple fact that you have been looking for a job for so long and, frankly, you are just tired of the whole process.

Wherever it comes from, fight it because the negative energy will be a distraction that will sap the positive elements of your presentation and seriously damage whatever chances you have to make a great impression.

Watch too for laziness and distractions—especially during the meeting. It might strike at any time due to information overload or distractions ("Is that really a Reynolds sculpture on the desk?) that cause you to stop listening. At the first signs, ward it off by reminding yourself not to let your guard down but to carefully listen to everything the interviewer is choosing to share with you. Don't let laziness prevent you from recording your notes right after the meeting because "you need a break." You might forget a very important piece of information that otherwise might have been included in the thank-you note that you waste no time in delivering. (See Figure 6-3.)

Last-Minute Checklist
to Help Beat the Competition

☐ **Be yourself.** Remember that they liked you on paper. Don't be a different person in person.

☐ **Be positive.** Keep reminding yourself of the key skills/requirements for the position and that you "have" them covered.

☐ **Don't be first.** If you can, schedule your interview for a Friday when more people are in a good mood. Try not to be the first candidate seen.

☐ **Don't shoot yourself in the foot.** Offering more information than is asked; talking just to fill up the silence; giving long, convoluted explanations will just underscore your lack of confidence.

☐ **Listen.** Really listen to what is said...and to what is not expressed verbally. Listen to what you are saying. Read body language clues.

☐ **Be flexible.** So the interviewer knows less about the company or the position than you do. Don't hit him/her over the head with it. Arrogance or impatience will not win him/her over, and that is one of the interview goals.

☐ **Be inquisitive.** Really want to learn about the organization, the job, and the hiring process.

☐ **Do not take it personally.** Hiring decisions can be quite subjective and even a matter of luck.

Figure 6-3

CHAPTER SEVEN

Defining Your Three Most Important Interview Goals

You have the interview appointment. You have chosen your clothing, completed your research, and brushed up on your etiquette. Now what? Granted that your overall goal is to obtain a fantastic job offer, but what do you want to accomplish in this particular interview? What are reasonable interview goals? Keep them brief, specific, and focused. We suggest that you have the following three interview goals:

- Make a succinct statement of what you bring to the job.
- Obtain detailed information so you can decide if you wish to further pursue the opportunity.
- Get the interviewer to want to hire you. (See Figure 7-1.)

Make your statement

An interview is an exchange of ideas, a sending and receiving of messages. What is the message you need to send? What do you want the interviewer to know about you as a candidate?

The interviewer needs to know the following:

- The skills you have that pertain to the job.
- Your experience(s) that provided the required skills.
- The people you worked with that influenced your career and/or your skills, if appropriate.
- What your personal job ethics and work methods are and how they compare with the organization's culture.

Interview Goals

1. Make your statement.
2. Obtain information.
3. Make them take action.

Figure 7-1

- What you know about the organization, the industry, the market, and the job.
- If you want the job.

In your research into this organization and the job opening, you should have discovered what their job requirements are and salient facts about the organization and the position. Is this a high-pressure job, or is more time allowed for decision making, for example? What are the basic job requirements? What is the organizational culture? What is the day-to-day workload? Your personal statement should address these areas.

What Do Interviewers Look for?

Knowing what an interviewer wants to hear can help you in forming the message that you send in an interview. All interviewers seemingly agree, even if they use different words, that they are looking for three main characteristics in a job candidate:

1. **Can do**: Proof that you can perform the job. You have done it before and can cite examples from your work history to prove it.
2. **Will do**: You are enthusiastic and motivated. You will perform in the job. You have the intangible passion to carry you through the mundane days as well as the problem situations; you have examples to share of when you have given the extra effort. You can and do learn.
3. **Fit**: You will fit into the existing team. You can prove that you have worked in similar organizations or teams settings and will be able to make a contribution quickly.

Whether it is a fast 15-minute interview or a 2-hour in-depth session, what are the points that you feel you must get across to the interviewer? Think marketing—you are the product. Why should they "buy" you? In priority order, list five key job requirements and proof that you can meet those requirements. (See Figure 7-2.)

For example, if you were interested in a position as a bank teller:

They need someone who is accurate with numbers and can handle currency and transactions; pleasant and helpful with customers.	• I am accurate with math and financial numbers and have been rated excellent. • I have taken bookkeeping and banking courses. • I have also worked three summers as a cashier in the same retail store. • My retail experience allowed for a great deal of customer contact.
Job requirement: Knowledge of MSWord and MSPublisher for small PR firm.	• I have worked extensively with both programs, designing brochures and graphics for ____ Inc. • I am able to import documents, scan materials, and establish templates for documents.

Job Requirement:	*Proof of my ability:*
1	1
2	2
3	3
4	4
5	5

Figure 7-2

The more instances where you can match *your skills* to *their requirements*, the more points you will score in an interview. Additionally, you will impress them with both your understanding of the job requirements as well as the research you have done. This will boost your confidence level.

The top five needs that you listed are your main selling points—the statement you want to make—and what the interviewer needs to know about you to offer you the job. Using the list of prioritized job requirements, make a statement about yourself. Imagine a one- or two-minute infomercial about the product you are selling—yourself.

> With my extensive training in word processing, combined with my graphic arts background, I have been able to create promotional pieces for the past two years for _____ Company that supported their launch of new services successfully. I have consistently met deadlines and budget requirements while producing work that is both creative and meets the specifics of the assignment.

Having made that statement, you are also now in a position to back up your claims with specific examples or situations from your past experience. Telling specific examples from your previous work experiences is a great way to elaborate or drive home a point. (See Figure 7-3.)

Obtain Information

Candidates often lose sight of the fact that they are judging the organization, determining what the job details are, and getting insight into the importance the organization places on its human assets and this job in particular. The organization and the interviewer are also being interviewed by you.

As you approach the facility, note the area and physical plant. Is it modern, up-to-date, or sorely in need of repairs? In the halls and elevators, be attuned to employee comments and conversations. Does it seem to be a good place to work? Are you treated well in the reception area? Are you expected? All of this is important and will factor in if a job is offered to you.

What do you need to know if a job is offered? What are the gaps in your information? Do you have a job description? If not, ask for one in advance. They will be impressed by your interest (and, if

---

Make Your Statement

_____
_____
_____
_____
_____
_____
_____
_____
_____
_____

Figure 7-3

they do not have one available, that is another nugget of information for you to file away). Do you know what department you would work in? Where does that department fit in the organization? Reporting relationships?

Make a list of facts that you have learned about the organization and the job and note the gaps in your information. This will form the outline for questions that you should ask in the interview IF you want to get the job offer (see Chapter 8—Preparing Your Own Questions.)

Use the outline in Figure 7-4 as a starting point for your information. You might find out more from your research (Chapter 5), or there might be other issues that are important to you and/or your career.

Make Them Take Action

What is the purpose of the interview? What do you want the interviewer to do? Are you testing the market, or do you really want this job? Is this a courtesy interview—someone referred you and you are seeing if there are any openings either now or in the future?

Information Worksheet

Name of Organization:

Corporation, partnership, nonprofit?

Minihistory: founded____ by whom_____ other facts:

Location:　Hqtrs:
　　　　　　Other/branches:

Employees:
　　　Union/nonunion?
Divisions/Departments:

Main Products/Services:

Major customers/clients/markets:

　　　Sample of ads?

Management:

Financial snapshot: Profitable? Growth? Recent developments?

Job description:

Title:

Department/Division:

Supervisor/Manager:

Major responsibilities/tasks:

Figure 7-4

Be very clear in your purpose for taking the interview. If you are seeking information or looking for further job leads, be certain that the interviewer is aware of this fact. The first step in getting them to offer you the job is to ask for it! It is surprising how many candidates leave the interview and never specifically state they are interested in the job and want to work there. Be prepared, however, to answer the interviewer's next logical questions if you have not already been asked:

Why do you want to work here?
Why should we hire you?

You can prepare more fully to answer these questions when you read Chapter 10.

Barring a love-at-first-sight reaction, the best you can reasonably hope for is a follow-up telephone call for a job offer or additional interviews. Before you leave the interview, ask what the next step will be. How soon do they plan to make a decision? Can you call them? Is there anything else they need? Ask for a business card.

You need to know what action they are planning and then schedule your follow-up accordingly. (For more on this topic, see Chapter 14—Thank You's and Follow Up.) Also see Figure 7-5.

Last-Minute Checklist
Job Search Wisdom

☐ **What you know is more important than whom you know.** Referrals are helpful in getting interviews, but it is your knowledge and your experience that will be evaluated. Don't be a name-dropper. If you hitch yourself to someone else's star, your career may rise and fall with theirs.

☐ **Prepare for the worst.** Always try to have contingency plans. Car not working? Can you get to interview with public transportation? Interviewer running behind schedule—how long can you wait? Can you reschedule?

☐ **Give and receive.** Be grateful for all help given and say so, in writing or verbally. Spread the wealth around. Had a great interview but job not for you? Know someone else who would be a better fit? Pass the word on.

☐ **Keep your sense of humor.** Do not take it all too seriously. Interviewing and job selection is highly subjective. If you can see the humor in potentially awkward situations, you can show that you can roll with the punches as well as feel better about yourself.

☐ **Be a lifelong learner.** Learn something new from every interview. Enjoy the people that you meet on your job search. Keep learning new skills, new tools to use, new ways to look at the world around you.

Figure 7-5

CHAPTER EIGHT

Preparing Your Own Questions

When preparing for an interview, no matter how long you have to get ready, it can be so easy to get overly concerned just with questions such as:

- What will the interviewer be like?
- Will he be impressed with my credentials?
- Will I have the "right" answers?
- Will I be considered for the job?

You should actually be focusing on:

- What kinds of people work here?
- What will it be like to work here?
- Whom will I report to?
- How will I be evaluated?

Why You Should Ask Questions

Earlier in the book we defined an interview as a conversation with a purpose. A conversation implies an exchange of information or ideas. Presuming that your goal is to get a job offer, what must you know to be able to evaluate the offer? What other information should you obtain during the course of the interview itself to further your candidacy? You should ask questions for three reasons:

1. To know enough to make a decision as to whether or not you want the job, if offered
2. To seize the opportunity to demonstrate your intelligence and responsiveness
3. To recognize any opportunity to respond with questions, and jump at the chance to do so

In researching the organization in advance of your interview, you will only be able to obtain so much information by virtue of both the time constraints and the type of organization. Publicly held companies will have more information available and written about them than privately owned companies. Regardless of the company's status, there will be gaps in your knowledge, some of it quite important to the interview and your overall understanding of what you are in for if you decide to join the organization. This is due to the simple fact that circumstance could always change at any moment. Just 10 minutes ago, for instance, a hostile takeover (or an indictment) could have been announced at a press briefing or to an online gathering of reporters.

How to Ask Questions

Before dealing with *what* to ask, it is important to know *how* to ask as well as *when* to bring up your questions. Always remain courteous and respectful; the fact that they have invited you for an interview shows their good judgment!

"*Why*" questions can appear judgmental because it can seem that you are asking them to justify certain actions or products. (This is also true when they ask questions of you, such as "*Why did you pick that course of study?*" or "*Why did you not get a graduate degree?*") It can be more effective to put your questions into context: "The *Wall Street Journal stated that you have recently divested yourself of several foreign affiliates; is there a plan to discontinue overseas production?*" This wording is immensely better than "*Why are you still operating those sweatshops overseas?*"

You do not appreciate being put on edge—take the same care when formulating your questions. Showing that you have done some research and that you are not idly curious will frame your queries nicely:

> I read in a recent *Wall Street Journal* that you had decided not to release the upgrade on your _____ because there were still bugs in the software. Do you mind sharing, if you can, how long the average time is from concept to release on typical software programs?

Raising a question such as this might prompt your being asked:

> "And why are you interested?"

You can then respond with:

> I have found that to be truly successful in sales, knowledge of the company's current and future operations is essential. If I hear that a new product is in the works, I can keep an eye peeled for

any changes in the market or in customer needs that would be helpful to other areas because I spend a lot of time in the field.

Interviewers might use a technique of creating a stressful environment for the candidate during their interview, but even if that happens, you should not appear aggressive. Strong, assured, confident, and unflappable are the key attributes to keep in mind. It is never good form to bring up organizational failures or scandals:

Gee, that product recall must have cost you a bunch.

Or

I was surprised to see that your CEO quit suddenly; was it really because he was about to be fired?

Salary, benefits, perks, and vacation schedules should wait until a firm job offer is made; many of those details should be contained in the written offer (see Chapter 16—Negotiate Offer).

What Questions You Should Ask and/or Could Ask

Consider the chart you prepared in the prior chapter (Figure 7-4). This chart of useful information can be a handy interview take-along to refer to before the interview as well as to help you fill in any blanks after the interview itself. It also provides the framework for questions for you to ask. (See Figure 8-1.)

Gear your questions to your audience. It would be great to have a personnel or HR rep who has intimate details of the job opening imbedded in his/her brain, ready for you to pick. Realistically, interviewers who are not part of the day-to-day operations of the area where you might work might not have anything but a rough outline or job description. Dealing with an interviewer who is ill equipped to answer even general questions about the job might be an indication of management's attitude toward the job, the department, or their employees in general. If appropriate, asking to meet with someone (ideally, the supervisor) would be a smart move.

Now comes the harder part—deciding which questions or information are important and why. Remember that the *most important part of the interview is to get your message across;* you should not turn it into a fact-finding mission regarding the organization's operations! But certain information can be crucial to your approach in the interview as well as evaluating any job offers. For example, there

What You Need to Know

Note your questions or missing information

Job Opening	
Organization	
Management	
Operations/ Financials	
Other (Deal Makers/ Breakers)	

Figure 8-1

are certain risks attendant to a start-up operation or one that has only been in business a short time. On the other end of the spectrum are organizations that have not had a new idea or product in decades. What kind of organization is interviewing you? Additionally, where they are in their time line might provide insight into their particular needs and culture.

Knowing the history of the organization is helpful to understand both where they have been and the direction they might be heading; all will better enable you and the interviewer to see you in the job. Another issue, and one that shows your sensitivity to the bottom line, are their revenue and income streams. How and where do they earn their money? Who are their customers? What economic factors affect their business? How have they been doing: earnings up, down, or flat? Any clues as to reasons for their income fluctuations—or why they have become stagnant?

Where are their markets? How do they market their goods or services? Who are their competitors? What are their key products? Any new products on the horizon? How might you support their future plans? Will you be working in a cost or profit center, and how can you contribute? (See Figure 8-2.)

You can see where this is going. Not all the pertinent facts can be found in a prospectus or even a detailed classified ad. If the interview was set up by a recruiter, even she might not have the whole picture. And, realistically, not every interviewer has all the details about the job opening. This can also be a big clue as to how serious the organization holds the post you are interviewing for. Are you being interviewed by someone in Personnel or by someone in the department where you will work? Can you meet your possible supervisor? See the department?

The general operations of the organization—its mission, performance, and future plans can also be explored. These are great open-ended questions to ask to elicit conversation and information. It also gives you a bit of a break, not being the subject of the interview.

Questions: Asked and Unasked

Not everything you need to know will be discovered through outright questioning. Many will be the result of observations. Even more can be learned from listening. If the interviewer is explaining the job description, listen for the details and see if you can flesh them out.

> You said this department had recently been reorganized. Can you elaborate on the reorganization for me?

Or

> If this position reports to the head of the department, I would really be interested in how the department fits into the organization as a whole.

Do not be afraid or hesitant to ask your own follow-up questions. If you do not understand a remark the interviewer has made,

Questions to Ask

- Where is job/department physically located? (In this building, another site?)
- How long has this position been vacant? Is it a new position?
- What happened to the last incumbent? (quit, fired, promoted?)
- When do you want to have the position filled?
- Who will make the hiring decision?
- What is the typical career path after this position?
- Whom would you report to? How report...verbally, written reports, and how often?
- What is the management style of organization?
- How many in department? Is it fully staffed at present?
- What is the average turnover/tenure in the department? In the organization?
- Is an organization chart available? Where does department fit into organization and its current mission?
- What has been/is the current operation of the department? On budget? Profitable? Costs under control?
- What does organization feel the biggest issue/problem in the department is? Future goals?
- Once I start, what do you feel would be my top priority?
- What do you think will be my biggest hurdle?
- Does the organization have a mission statement?
- What kinds of employee achievements are recognized?
- Can you describe the environment here?
- What does it take for someone to be successful here?

Figure 8-2

ask for clarification. Should an interesting fact about the job or the organization be mentioned, ask for more information.

> You mentioned the company was going to change over to using the _____ operating system. I am very interested in the process that led up to that decision. I am familiar with that system as well as ____ and ____.

Whether it is a tacit understanding or the interviewer states it directly, information gleaned from the interview—from statements and/or observations—remains confidential. If you feel that you are privy to unreleased information, it is a nice touch to comment on it.

> I appreciate being allowed to see your new assembly line before it is put into production and will treat this information confidentially.

Observations

What you see and hear can be more insightful than a corporate report. Many candidates are not hired because the interviewer feels they will not fit into the organizational culture. This is also one of the prime reasons for employees being encouraged to leave employment or termination: that illusive "fit." Since most states are "at will" employment states (meaning that employees can be let go for a good reason, a bad reason, or no reason at all—as long as it is not for an illegal reason), the entire interview process can be subjective on both sides. You might project some indefinable quality that appeals to the interviewer or not; the same is true of your impressions of the interviewer and the organization. The vibes might just tell you very clearly that this is not a place where you want to spend a lot of time!

From the moment of your arrival for your interview, be observant. Discreetly take notes, if possible, before you go into your meeting. What clues to the culture, the organization can you glean from merely arriving for your meeting? (See Figure 8-3.)

Deal Makers and Deal Breakers

An initial interview is *not* the opportunity to discuss salary, benefits, or vacation time. Those subjects should be dealt with when a job offer is made. There are times when the salary is disclosed up front, by the interviewer, in the advertisement for the job opening, stated

Interview Observations

- Where was organization located? (own building, offices elsewhere).
- Was the signage clear? Organization's name displayed?
- Building in good repair? Construction going on? Active location?
- Reception area well lit, comfortably appointed?
- What was on the walls?

  Posters for softball practice, sign-ups for training classes?

  Photos of employee activities, teams?
- Organizational literature, posters, ads displayed?
- Did the receptionist expect you? Was your arrival announced?
- Were you treated professionally, in a businesslike manner?
- Where were interview offices located?
- Was there privacy for interview?
- Was interviewer prepared? Share knowledge of organization? Knowledge of job requirements?
- Were you able to see your prospective work area?

  What was condition of work area?

  Other areas?

  Were employees in cubicles, offices, or open areas?
- What was your impression of any other employees you saw?
- Does it appear to be a "family friendly" place? Is it a social as well as professional environment?

Figure 8-3

by the recruiter or discovered in the course of your research (you know someone in the organization).

As important as compensation and benefits are to you, there might be other areas that play an important part in your choice of jobs. You might have had your fill of start-up organizations, or perhaps you are not interested in a staid, conservative organization. Make sure you find out if travel is a part of the job, especially if you are not interested in traveling at this point in your life. If these facts were not discovered in your research, the interview is the time to flush them out. Be on the lookout for brochures that outline their employee benefits or programs available in the reception area.

Other than salary and benefits, what else about the organization and/or the position would influence your accepting a job offer? *Note:* these facts might be best covered in a callback or second interview and might be points of negotiation when a firm offer is made. See Chapter 16 for a more comprehensive discussion.

What Should You Do with Their Answers?

As soon as possible after you exit the interview, take notes. You have your basic fact sheet and can now fill in some if not all of the blanks.

Why fill out a fact sheet? In order to write a personalized thank-you note, for example. And, should they call you back for another interview, you can refresh your memory and do additional research. All of this is so that you can make an informed decision if and when a job offer is extended. (See Figure 8-4.)

Last-Minute Checklist
Quick Question Tips

☐ Know where you are going before you start a topic or line of questions. If you bring up a subject, be prepared to handle any follow-up questions the interviewer may raise.

☐ Don't ask questions that you should already know or have discovered before the interview. If the organization was in the headlines this morning, won't you feel foolish admitting you never read the papers or listened to news today and know nothing about the recent events?

☐ Enjoy the silence. Once you have answered, be quiet. Use the tactic on the interviewer—maybe he or she will continue with additional information if you do not immediately jump in.

☐ You are protected from illegal discrimination—steer clear of those topics yourself.

Figure 8-4

The Interview

CHAPTER NINE

The Five Stages of the Interview

There are as many different types of interviews as there are different types of interviewers, but there are some consistencies in the shape of each interview. Think about when you have been introduced to someone for the first time. You chat, trying to find some common bonds. Then you explore those common interests, getting more and more deeply into the subject as time allows. At the end, you and the other person decide if the budding friendship will be pursued. "Get together for coffee sometime?" Business cards or telephone numbers might be exchanged (or not). Sincere good-byes, nice-to-meet-you's might be traded or you might just go through the polite motions, not interested in seeing this person again. Just like dating. Just like an interview.

Before the Interview Starts

You might be asked to complete an application while you are waiting for your appointment. You might have been told this in advance, or it could be so routine for them that they do not even mention it.

It might be an application that you fill out with a pen or pencil. Or, with some technologically advanced organizations, you might be seated in front of a computer monitor and asked to complete a form generated by a software program. If you are not comfortable using computers and keyboards, that can be a daunting experience. However, if you are interviewing with a high-tech or even technologically evolved organization, familiarity with computers and Internet know-how is likely to be expected of you.

The interviewer might have a copy of the application form together with your resume in front of him/her to refer to, so please make the facts consistent. (Now, aren't you glad you completed the detailed Employment History we urged you to do in Chapter 3?) Fill in the requested information and, if asked for references, list those that you have already obtained permission to list. And notice what the interviewer does with your application; their actions can tell you a lot. One applicant, after being surprised with being asked to complete an application form, was stymied when the interviewer never collected it! That was an obvious sign that the candidacy was not going to be pursued by the organization! (See Figure 9-1.)

Application For Employment

PLEASE WRITE PLAINLY OR PRINT

REFERRAL SOURCE

☐ ADVERTISEMENT   ☐ EMPLOYMENT AGENCY

(Name of Publication)   (Name of Agency)

☐ EMPLOYEE REFERRAL: ☐ OTHER:

(Name of employee)

PERSONAL INFORMATION

NAME   Last   First   Middle   Social Security Number   Date

ADDRESS   Street and Number   Apt.   City   State   Zip Code

TELEPHONE   Area Code   Exchange   Number   Are you legally entitled to work in this country? ☐ Yes ☐ No
If yes and you are not a U.S. Citizen, enter your Alien Registration No.

Are you over 17 years of age?   ☐ Yes   ☐ No

List any additional information relative to former last name and/or nickname necessary for educational or business reference checks:

EMPLOYMENT INFORMATION

Position applied for: ☐ Full Time   ☐ Vacation Relief
    ☐ Part Time   ☐ Temporary

Salary desired   When can you start work?

Are you willing to work overtime if scheduled?   ☐ Yes   ☐ No

Are there any reasons why you will be unable to work certain hours or days for other than religious reasons?   ☐ Yes   ☐ No   If "Yes" please explain.

Have you ever applied for a position with Bank of Ireland or its divisions and subsidiaries?   ☐ Yes   ☐ No   If "Yes" please explain.

PRESENT OR LAST EMPLOYER
This Section Must Be Completed Even If Supplemented By A Resume
(List Applicable Military Or Volunteer Experiences)

Name of Company   Type of Business

Address   Street and Number   City   State   Zip Code   Telephone

Title of Job   Employed: From: Mo.   Yr.   To: Mo.   Yr.   Starting Rate   Present or Last Rate

Description of Work

Name of Your Supervisor   Supervisor's Title

Reason for Leaving   May we consult your employer? ☐ Yes ☐ No

GA-93-8/85-1M

Figure 9-1

NEXT TO LAST EMPLOYER (List Other Employers in Similar Order)						
Name of Company				Type of Business		
Address	Street and Number	City	State		Zip Code	Telephone
Title of Job		Employed: From: Mo. Yr.	To: Mo. Yr.	Starting Rate		Last Rate
Description of Work						
Name of Your Supervisor			Supervisor's Title			
Reason for Leaving						

Name of Company				Type of Business		
Address	Street and Number	City	State		Zip Code	Telephone
Title of Job		Employed: From: Mo. Yr.	To: Mo. Yr.	Starting Rate		Last Rate
Description of Work						
Name of Your Supervisor			Supervisor's Title			
Reason for Leaving						

Name of Company				Type of Business		
Address	Street and Number	City	State		Zip Code	Telephone
Title of Job		Employed: From: Mo. Yr.	To: Mo. Yr.	Starting Rate		Last Rate
Description of Work						
Name of Your Supervisor			Supervisor's Title			
Reason for Leaving						

IF ABOVE DOES NOT INCLUDE ALL JOBS SINCE YOU STARTED WORKING, PLEASE LIST OTHERS BELOW			
COMPANY	JOB	FROM	TO

PLEASE EXPLAIN ALL PERIODS OF UNEMPLOYMENT OF MORE THAN TWO WEEKS DURATION SINCE COMPLETION OF FORMAL EDUCATION		
FROM	TO	REASON FOR UNEMPLOYMENT

Figure 9-1 (Continued)

OCCUPATIONAL QUALIFICATIONS

TYPING _____ W.P.M.   SHORTHAND _____ W.P.M.

List business machines you can operate or other office skills relevant to position desired.

Other skills:

FOREIGN LANGUAGES	Speak:	Read:	Write:

EDUCATION

Circle Highest Grade or Year Completed At Each Level	Name of School	City	State	Dates From To	Degree or Diploma
High School 1 2 3 4					
Technical School 1 2 3 4					
College 1 2 3 4					
Graduate School 1 2 3 4					

College   Major _____

Minor _____   _____ First ¼_____ Sec ¼_____ Third ¼_____ Fourth ¼

Graduate School   Major _____

Minor _____

Technical School   Course _____   _____ First ¼_____ Sec ¼_____ Third ¼_____ Fourth ¼

Class Standing—Please Check

What subjects have you taken in school or since leaving school which will be helpful in the work for which you are applying?

List Academic Honors or Scholarships

Indicate what you do in your spare time that would help you in the position you are applying for.

Figure 9-1 (Continued)

GENERAL INFORMATION

NAMES OF FRIENDS AND RELATIVES EMPLOYED BY _____ OR A SUBSIDIARY

NAME	POSITION AND RELATIONSHIP	LOCATION

LIST PREVIOUS ADDRESS (ONLY IF DURING LAST 10 YEARS)

STREET	CITY	STATE	FROM	TO

Please provide any additional information which you believe to be related to making a hiring decision for the job for which you have applied.

HEALTH: Do you have any impairments, physical, mental, or medical which would interfere with your ability to perform the job for which you have applied? If there are any positions or types of positions for which you should not be considered, or job duties you cannot perform because of a physical, mental, or medical disability, please describe. (NOTE: The Bank is committed to make reasonable accommodation to disabilities pursuant to the Rehabilitation Act of 1973.)

Have you ever been convicted of a crime other than a minor traffic violation? ☐ Yes ☐ No   If answer is "Yes," please explain.

Federal and/or State and City law prohibit discrimination in hiring and employment on the basis of race, color, religion, national origin, sex, age, marital status, handicap, and disability or Vietnam-era veteran status. No question on this application is intended to secure information to be used for such discrimination and your opportunity for employment will be based solely on your merit and on no other consideration.

I hereby authorize _____, its subsidiaries, and/or its agents or representatives to investigate or cause an investigation to be made of my education and employment experience and all other aspects of my background relevant to my proposed employment, including all statements made by me in my application for employment. I understand that any job offer is contingent upon receipt by _____ of employment references acceptable to the Bank. I also agree to release _____ its subsidiaries and/or its agents or representatives, as well as any person to whom such inquiry is directed, from any liability arising directly or indirectly from such investigation.

I certify that the information contained herein is accurate and complete to the best of my knowledge and understand that any misrepresentation of fact may be considered sufficient reason for withdrawal of an offer of employment or subsequent dismissal if employed.

If employed, I agree to abide by the rules and regulations of the ____ and I recognize that either I or the ____ may terminate my employment at any time for reasons other than those specifically prohibited by law.

This form is intended for use throughout the United States.

Signature of Candidate _____ Date _____

REFERRAL RECORD

Supervisor	Dept.	Date	Accepted	Rate	Starting Date	Rejected

Figure 9-1 (Continued)

Greeting/Small Talk

For some of us, the first five minutes is the worst part of the interview or of any conversation. The ability to make small talk might seem inconsequential but can set the tone of the entire process. It can show how comfortable both parties are with their roles, as well as break the ice for the interview itself. It can give insight into the organization's culture and indicate how serious they take hiring employees.

Generally, the job candidate will follow the lead of the interviewer. Shake hands if a hand is extended, and exchange names and pleasantries. You might say something like:

> Miss Hanson, I am so glad you were able to set up this interview on such short notice. The position of copy editor at _____ is one that I feel that I am well suited for.

If questioned, now is not the time or place to rail against all the construction delays you were surprised with nor comment on any news headlines. ("How about those Yankees?" "Ooops. You are a Mets fan?") You never know where the interviewers' loyalties or biases lie. "All is good" is a great frame of mind to maintain. You had no problems finding the office, everyone has been helpful, you are confident that you will do a great job when hired, and you are simply delighted to be there!

Offer your business card (and hope you are given one in exchange!) together with a recent copy of your resume. Sit attentively and comfortably; enjoy the process.

Setting the Parameters

There are many types of interviewers and interviews. Some interviewers are well prepared and expert in leading you through your "story," while others seem to have awoken that morning having no idea about the interview process or your interest in a job with the organization. You hope for the former and but should be prepared to deal with the latter. (See Figure 9-2.)

Regardless of the type of interviewer, the first rule in setting the parameters is to listen. And that means active listening—participating in the exchange of information. We spend years learning to read and write, yet very little time is spent on learning how to listen. As discussed in Chapter 4, listening is different than hearing. How often, when you

Types of Interviewers	How to Deal with Them
• Well prepared, articulate, listens actively, understands the job opening and offers insights to organization.	• Enjoy it! You have an expert interviewer.
• Unprepared	• Restate reason for interview, what position you are interested in, your qualifications; offer copy of resume.
• Only asks "yes-no" questions	• Whenever it is important, elaborate briefly. These types of questions often suggest "right" answer: *"Do you plan your day ahead of time?"*
• Constantly chatters on about subjects other than the purpose of the interview	• Be polite but try as well as you can to redirect interview. *"Yes, I can see how much sky-diving interests you. I can relate because graphic design interests me the same way, which is why I feel I am quite qualified for the position."*
• Allows frequent interruptions (telephone calls, door kept open)	• Suggest a less-busy time to reschedule. If still persists in running interview, make the best of it and get as many of your points across. Ask *"Is this the normal pace of business here?"* to gain some insight into company.

Figure 9-2

are introduced to someone new, do you listen to hear your own name pronounced correctly and totally forget the name of the person you just met? Watch any good televised talk show (not the ones with all the yelling and screaming); the host engages the guest. There is body language, gestures, and listening. Just being aware of this aspect of the interview will improve your performance. (See Figure 9-3.)

Be an Effective Listener

- Be calm—leave emotions outside the interview room.
- Be polite but not overawed or subservient.
- Do not assume anything.
- Do not interrupt.
- Pay attention. Do not get distracted.
- Make eye contact but do not stare.
- Be aware of body language. Good posture enforces attention.
- Slow it down. Do not rush to speak.
- Modulate your voice. Avoid mumbling, "up" speak or using fillers "ummm," "like," "you know."
- Offer feedback; give verbal and nonverbal clues that you are listening.
- Use appropriate language. Avoid jargon, arcane, or grandiose words. Resemble your resume and cover letter.

Figure 9-3

The Main Event

This is the event for which you have been preparing since you found out about this interview. You know what your message is—what your goals are in this interview (see Chapter 7).

No matter what type of interviewer you have, there are different types of interview formats. You might be shuttled from Personnel/Human Resources to a department head or to a supervisor for additional interviews in the same day. You might sit across the desk from one individual or face several interviewers at the same time. In some cases, you might not be the sole interviewee. It might be a group interview. It is a "casting call" to eliminate some candidates while choosing to focus on others in further interviews. You might know this in advance or—Surprise! (This is why research is so important. Knowing someone who works there now or who has worked or interviewed there recently can provide invaluable insights not only into the organization but also into the hiring process.) (See Figure 9-4.)

The Questions!

There are four types of questions you will face:

1. Questions that you are glad they asked; these are the ones that let you state your message.

2. Questions that you hoped they would not ask—ones that expose those skeletons in your closet. These are the ones that you find it difficult to answer. (See Chapter 11.)

3. Questions that they should not ask. These are illegal and relate to those areas protected by federal, state, or local laws. (See Chapter 10.)

4. Questions that you (or we) never anticipated. Seemingly totally irrelevant questions. Remember, interviews are subjective. Who knows what book the interviewer read recently to give him/her the idea for "perfect" interview questions?

Easy Questions

You want to share your successes, your achievements, and your skills. This is what you spent hours preparing for. If your interviewers do not seek these answers, you have to interject them into your narrative yourself. These are the highlights of your cover/marketing letter, the main thrust of your resume and the reasons why they should hire you.

> You asked about what software I was familiar with but did you notice on my resume that I was part of a team that helped to develop the _____ software that is now in beta production?

Or:

> Not only is my typing speed well over 70 wpm, but also I have a working knowledge of word processing and desktop publishing. In my prior position, I was responsible for preparing all the district sales reports for the quarterly meetings. Management complimented me on both the accuracy and the visual layout of these documents.

Types of Interviews

Purpose

Courtesy Interview: Exactly as it sounds; you are being interviewed as a favor to someone. There might or might not be a job opening.

Recruiting Interview: Attract possible candidates.

Screening Interview: Culling out the candidates that fit the qualifications. You must pass this hurdle before going on to further interviews.

Selection Interview: Talking with hiring manager to fill the position. This is what is typically thought of as a job interview.

Hiring Interview: Make job offer and negotiate terms.

Format

Face-to-face: personal interaction in the same location

Remote: by telephone, videoconferencing, computer

Written: by e-mail or traditional mail; forms

Panel: interviewed by a group at the same time

Group: several candidates are interviewed at the same time

Approach

Structured: Fill in the blanks, formatted questions

Unstructured: Free form "Tell me about yourself..."

Situational: Asks *"What if..."* type of questions

Behavioral: Poses "Tell me about a time when..."

Case Study: Solving problems or resolving situations

Stress: Antagonistic questions; tries to push buttons

Combination: any or all of the above.

Figure 9-4

Hard Questions

Your work or educational background might have some soft spots. First, get over it. If you did not think that you are a great candidate for this position, you would not be there. Second, interviewers have heard it all before. If you have had a problem in your past and it is part of your work record, best to reveal it and get past it.

> Yes, at _____ I was let go after a particularly poor sales period. They released 15 percent of their sales force. Because I was a new hire and had not had the opportunity to prove myself, I was one of the first to be laid off. However, in the short time I was with them, I did obtain some valuable insights into the marketplace. In a soft economy, I feel that _____.

Make your explanation very matter of fact and then move on to some positive aspect such as being available now for this terrific position at this great organization. "*It is all good.*"

Illegal Questions

It might be hard to believe that with all the information disseminated that any interviewer would ask a patently illegal question in an interview. Should they do so, you might or might not react in a polite manner to the blunder. "*I am sorry, but are you saying that my marital status is a job requirement?*"

Regardless of the interviewer's motivation, you might wish to answer a question that is illegal because it would further your candidacy.

> Actually, I still do wear my wedding ring even though recently divorced. It was an amicable arrangement, and I am looking forward to moving on with my life. The position here is an excellent opportunity for me to relocate.

Or:

> Yes, I am Japanese and speak the language fluently. I am also fluent in German, Russian, Italian, Spanish, and Mandarin. Global economics is a major influence in today's business don't you think? You have offices overseas in three or four countries, I believe.

Or even:

I already have two other children and am fortunate to have had
live-in child care for the past five years provided by a close relative. I have had an outstanding attendance record the past two
years with my current employer, taking only a few days off for the
birth of my last child.

State, local, and federal laws protect against discrimination in
certain categories in employment. The categories protected by federal laws include: race, color, religion, national origin, gender
(including pregnancy), age (40 and over), disabilities, and Vietnam-
era veterans. State and local statutes sometimes extend protection
for sexual orientation and lower the protected age category to 18.
(See Chapter 11 for further information on illegal questions.)

Your Turn to Ask Questions

You have your list of questions and topics to explore that you prepared in Chapter 8. You have kept your eyes and ears open before
and during the interview. You have inserted some queries in the
course of the interview as opportunity and topics presented themselves. Now, the interviewer looks at you and asks: *"Do you have any
questions?"* Well, do you?

If you have had an excellent interviewer and truly covered all
that you were interested in, then state so.

I had researched ____ before our meeting but had been unable
to find out about ____. I really appreciate your explaining the
current procedure and future expansion plans. The ____ aspect
was particularly intriguing, and I will certainly follow ____
progress in the trade papers. Is there anything else you need to
know from me?

Or

Your description of the department was excellent and gave me
a picture of how it fits into the organization as a whole. If I
am being considered for the position, may I have a tour of
the area?

In all circumstances, always be sure to avoid making the weakest response:

Not really. You have been answering all my questions throughout the interview.

Closing

No, this is not the time to beat a hasty retreat. This should not have been an ordeal, but a pleasant learning experience for both parties. Basically, there are three items left to cover:

1. Thank the interviewer for her time. A simple and sincere "Thank you for your time and all the information "will suffice. Shaking hands and using the interviewer's name are also nice touches. If there was something that came up in the interview, follow up with a promise to send an article or brochure. "I will not forget that article we discussed from *Information Weekly*. I will look for it online."

   Ask if there is anything else that you might add to help your candidacy. "Is there any other information you need to support my candidacy? I hope I have left you with an understanding of my skills and experience." Or: *"After our discussion, is there anything else I can tell you that would favorably support my candidacy?"*

2. Ask for the job. This is the one thing many interviewees fail to do. If you are interested in the position say so. "You have presented me with a clear understanding of the organization and the position. With my experience in ____, I feel that I could quickly add value to the organization and am very excited about the possibility of working here."

3. Understand what the next steps will be. "You stated you would like to fill the position by the end of next month. May I call you in two weeks to check on the status of my candidacy?" Or: "I understand that you have only just begun the process to fill the position. When would you like to see it filled?"

And, with that, your interview is finished. Congratulations! Making it through with flying colors is something to be proud of, even if you don't take the job. (See Figure 9-5.)

Last-Minute Checklist

Interview Success Tips

- ☐ Focus and refocus attention on your successes.
- ☐ Always offer positive information.
- ☐ Discuss only the facts needed to answer the question.
- ☐ Listen carefully.
- ☐ If you do not understand the question or point raised, ask for clarification.
- ☐ Tell the truth but do not offer information not asked for.
- ☐ Make your points. Then ask if interviewer would like further details.
- ☐ Be organized in your presentation.
- ☐ Be concise in your responses.
- ☐ Do not open doors to areas you would rather not discuss.
- ☐ Pause at times to consider your responses.

And remember—You are prepared.

There is no question you cannot answer, even if it is to say *"I do not know but I can get back to you."*

You know your skills and know you can do the job.

You know how and when you will add value to the organization.

Figure 9-5

CHAPTER TEN

Preparing Your Answers

People get jobs by being effective communicators during the interview process. In this chapter, we discuss practical ways to influence your interviewer by carefully answering his/her questions throughout the interview process. Preparation, passion, spontaneity, and preparation (so important we include it twice) are all keys to successful interviewing.

As we start this chapter, also think in terms of brief, engaging storytelling. First, you need to be sure you are a storyteller—not one who dreams up tales—but one who in a very brief and interesting way is able to share experiences that will easily hold the listener's attention.

Second, even though the interview might easily be seen in a "question-answer, question-answer, question-answer" format, the most effective interviews are conversations where the interviewer and the applicant—seamlessly glide through the meeting. The result is that both the interviewer and the applicant succeed in obtaining the information they need to come to a decision (don't forget you are there to make a decision as well: Do you want to work there?) and do it in a most pleasing manner for both parties.

Regardless of the response, remember to be brief. (Rule of thumb: if your listener breaks eye contact, you have gone on too long.)

A Warning—Do Not Overprepare!

As the time for that scheduled interview draws closer, you need to be careful that you do not overprepare. Be as confident as you can be from the preparation you do, but be careful that your responses are fresh and crisp—even though you might have gone over them several times as you prepared and rehearsed for this interview. Just as in any performance, even though you have been through this a lot, the interviewer is seeing you for the first time. And remember that even in subsequent visits to the same organization, you will continually be meeting new people—all for the first time!

Preparing versus Rehearsing—
You Need Both

Note the difference between preparing and rehearsing. When you prepare answers for your interview, you are reviewing your professional history, specific work experiences, and on-the-job successes and failures— so that you are able to discuss yourself succinctly and comprehensively in your interview.

Your rehearsal (and one of the three big "Rs") consists of practicing your presentation in a question-and-answer format so that your material is offered most effectively, holding the attention of the interviewer, who will be persuaded by your response to conclude that you are by far the best candidate for the job.

Discussing Your Accomplishments Is the
Way to Get an Offer

Remember that frequently job seekers are reluctant to talk about themselves because they don't want to appear to be boasting. We have usually been taught as we were growing up that we should never boast. The interviewer, however, needs to know your accomplishments in order to know that you are the right person for the job. So boast away!

Another reason you need to prepare and rehearse is to learn to separate your accomplishments from those of your team. If you have been an active participant in one or more team sports, the concept was reinforced whenever there were victories to share— regardless the level of competition. Throughout U.S. history, women had a role that kept them, until most recently, in the shadows, and they were encouraged to glow in the glory of their male colleagues.

Now in an interview, regardless of your gender and your past as a team player, you are required, on your own, to share your experiences, including your accomplishments, if you want to position yourself to be given a job offer. No one else can help you at that interview. Remember, too, that there are others—friends or family, perhaps— who certainly can assist you beforehand with your preparation and your rehearsal. Take the time to really prepare and ask for assistance to ensure that your answers are the greatest and are endorsed by one or even more persons whose opinions you will value.

Targeting your Responses

The first step in preparing your answers is reviewing the topics that you should be ready to discuss in any interview. See Figure 10-1 to review all the areas that you should be ready to discuss, providing details when necessary.

The second step is targeting your answers for the specific job that you seek. Before we continue, though, let's take a moment to recall the old joke of the person who approaches another, who happens to be standing with a dog. When the question is raised "Does your dog bite?" and the answer given is no, the person bends down to pet the dog. As this action takes place and the dog bites the petter, the person just bitten annoyingly remarks, "I thought you said your dog doesn't bite?" The other replies, "I did, but that isn't my dog."

That joke is particularly relevant here because you need to be extremely careful that each and every response you make is listener directed. Watch out, if you are making small talk, to not comment about pictures of kids that you see on the desk or golf clubs in the corner (remember: you might not even be the interviewer's office).

Both resumes and interviews need to be seen as marketing tools that are driven by the demands, requirements, and needs of the interviewer. One of the lighter aspects of professional life is when recent college graduates, who have yet to hold a full-time job beyond summer break, send human resource departments resumes that are two or three pages long. Another mistake occurs when resumes from those same individuals, a few years later, arrive that still include GPA's (grade point averages) and extracurricular activities—sometimes in great detail—when those alumni should replace that outdated information with demonstrations of very professional credentials instead. In "pre-PC-with-laser-printer" days, the most popular form of resume was the version that was printed at great expense by a commercial printing firm, so you were restricted to the same resume regardless of circumstances.

Now, with so much technology available at a very affordable price, it is inexcusable to have just one unchanged resume for all your job search pursuits. Your resume should be tailored—not by twisting facts but by emphasizing skills and accomplishments that might be more appropriate to your pursuit of one job and not so much for another.

Subjects You Should Be Ready to Discuss at Every Interview

All and any of the categories below might be explored during any interview:

- **Education.** Where have you gone? Degrees held? Why? What are you learning at this time?

- **Work history.** Who, what, where, why, when, and for what pay? Has there been a career plan? Promotions?

- **Skills.** What do you have? To what extent? Are they the skills the organization needs now? How are you keeping up to date?

- **Experience.** How is it related to the current position? Can you apply here what you have done elsewhere? Will you be able to teach others?

- **Personal characteristics.** Who are you? What are your interests, goals, strengths, weaknesses, plans, aspirations, failures, and achievements? Do you want to join us? Can we believe you?

- **Your Marketing Package.** What exactly are you selling? Why are you selling to us? How much will you cost? Do we need you and your skills? How can we best use you?

- **The organization and the job.**
  — Who are they?
  — What business are they in?
  — What is their mission, values?
  — What are the all-inclusive requirements of the job?
  — Is there any opportunity for personal and professional growth?
  — What are the challenges of the job at this time?

Figure 10-1

You should also tailor your approach to each interview. To ensure that you are most effectively prepared—especially when you just have just 24 hours to do it—you should have a customized set of answers that you expect and/or want to be asked. And you should be as ready as you can be with the answers. We will discuss how to identify those answers below. You will also see how to be best prepared for them when they are raised. We will also briefly discuss how to deal with questions that you would prefer not be asked. Last, we will discuss how you will be able to insert your answers, when you wish to, into your engaging conversation—even when those questions have not been raised.

Basic Research: Who They Are, What They Need, What You Offer

Disclosure/Control

Before we discuss the answers in more detail, let's be sure you understand two essential elements of every interview—disclosure and control.

Disclosure refers to how much information to share with the interviewer, as well as when to do it. You want to be careful to share no more information than you need to, and at the best possible time to do so. Consider the following examples. When asked, "Why did you leave your last job?" you have little choice of timing because a direct question has just been asked. But you still have complete control over what you choose to disclose (unless of course you shared the reason somewhere else—it might even have been in your cover letter). The real reason you might have left is that your boss was the worst and the organization was the stingiest and you might really want to share that piece of information.

Before you proceed, take a moment to realize that the job you are fighting for might have an even worse boss and the organization you are joining might be even more frugal. Alternatively, you might say, "The commute was the worst." Well, where is this organization located, and how difficult will it be for you to get here? The fact is that as intolerable (or even if it wasn't so bad) as your last employer was, there are usually several reasons, especially in a very uncertain market, for taking the chance and leaving one employer to seek another because it is a major decision. Consider other reasons to disclose to the interviewer without getting into the personality of your detested boss or the stinginess of the organization. "I decided to leave because the company was in a downsizing mode and I did not see career opportunities any longer. If I stayed, I would never have had the opportunity to look for another job because we, as survivors, were expected to do more with less." That is a *controlled* answer. Hold those "I hated that situation because..." comments for some other time and place. No one is going to hire a whiner.

Honesty or Obfuscation?

Be careful as you go through the facts that the picture you are portraying is a credible one. When a contentious issue, such as pay, is raised, be careful not to be suspected of hiding something. We discuss the topic of pay below and how to handle it whenever it might arise. It is important to remember to be careful with what you choose to disclose and when you choose to disclose it. Any topics that will have an impact when an offer is made and negotiated should not be handicapped by information sought by any of the interviewers earlier. You don't want to give them an advantage for use in the negotiation stage.

Questions You Want to Be Asked or That Need to Be Asked

There are questions that you want to be asked or that need to be asked so that you get a chance to provide the answers you want the interviewer to hear to prove you are the perfect person for the job.

We are talking about control. In every interview, the interviewer should be the one who establishes and maintains control throughout the meeting. Sometimes you will come across those who are really proficient at conducting an interview and at other times, you will run into those who aren't at all skilled at interviewing. More frequently you will deal with interviewers who, although not superstars, are competent. In any of these instances—regardless the skill level of the interviewer—you need to determine what you must do to ensure that the interviewer leaves the meeting with the information that you have concluded in advance is essential to your being brought back for additional meetings and, ultimately, a job offer. An example would be, "I really have not had recent experience in ____, but let me mention to you that I did take a leadership role in the _____ project. Is that exposure going to be of assistance to you here?"

How to Lose Control

You lose control during the interview when you provide information that will allow the interviewer to proceed down paths that are difficult for you. "I left my last job because I was part of a major downsizing due to changing economic conditions" is a pretty tight response to the question of why you left your last job. This answer seems organizationally based, and you were just swept up in the terminations as the staff was reduced. You were merely in the wrong place at the wrong time.

On the other hand, "I left over a policy dispute" just begs for additional information that you are unable to prevent from passing on until the listener feels she has heard enough. You have just lost control with this disclosure. Consider the following response, "I would love to work for this organization because it appears to have much better benefits than my current employer." By making that statement, you leave yourself open to three paths of questions. First, "What makes you say that?" Second, "Are you switching employers because of the benefits?" Third, "That is quite a comment you make because our employees who decide to leave us for your organization make the same comment. What is it about our benefits that you feel are better than those offered to you at this time?"

In each of these instances you have lost control due to your own answers, and you will be unable to end any discussion about them until the interviewer has had enough.

Below are answers to the questions that you need to be ready for. The list is not intended to be all-inclusive, but it is a complete one—that is, if you are ready with these answers, you will be comprehensively prepared for the question-and-answer format that you might expect.

All of your answers should reflect in tone, as well as content, that you are confident you are able to do the job (can do), excited by the prospect (will do) of working for this organization, and a great person to have around each and every day (fit).

Elevator Pitch (Formerly "Tell Me about Yourself")

Always have prepared what is currently called an "elevator pitch." It is a 30-second (or less) response to the "tell me about yourself" question. It is a succinct summary that defines who you are, what you have done, and where you are in your career.

> I am a proven marketing professional with more than 10 years' experience in consumer products. I have a record of targets met or surpassed in highly competitive settings. I am searching for an opportunity to put those skills to challenging use again. Please tell me what aspect of my past professional experiences you would like me to discuss in more detail.

When given the opportunity to give this answer, you can accomplish two things immediately. First, you set the tone by demonstrating that you can offer crisp, brief statements. Second, you can attempt right from the start to engage the interviewer in a dialogue rather than a question and answer session.

Answers to Demonstrate That You Can Do This Job

As discussed in Chapter 5, your preparation for the interview should include a careful review of any information that you have about the job you are being considered for. Be it a newspaper ad, Internet posting, or comments from a recruiter or colleague—review everything you have regarding what the job requires and what skills and knowledge you have that meets those needs. Use their language when you can. For example, if the organization refers to its employees as associates, always do the same. If you are interviewing for a corporate job at MacDonald's, be sure to refer to their fast food outlets as restaurants because they do.

Answers to Demonstrate You Know the Organization

"What do you know about us?" is a very fair question for potential employers to ask—regardless of the function and job for which you are applying. Some professions and occupations have a poor reputation for "thinking outside the box" when it comes to any level of understanding of the business. Others have a great reputation.

Accounting folks are more likely to understand and be sensitive to the nature of the organization from a business standpoint. Day in and day out, they are relied upon by executives, shareholders, and the marketplace to know the financial information they are responsible for providing. Whether it is a dot.com selling online ads or a hospital, accounting and finance professionals will be sensitive to the success or failure of products or services the organization provides due to payments from the customers/clients/patients who are the recipients. Finance and accounting professionals also have the advantage of always knowing the financial condition of the organization from the calls that it does or does not receive on a regular basis. If the organization is paying its bills slowly or are not being paid at all, the calls will come to accounts payable. If cash flow is surging, they will be the first to know about it from a daily review of deposits and payments.

Other functions, such as Information Technology, Human Resources, and Legal should make an effort to be sure they are aware of what the organization does, develop an understanding of the business it is in, and make a conscientious effort to know the organization's financial condition at all times as well. The problem starts when there is a perception that the professional expertise for the specific functional area is universal. "Human Resources is the same regardless the organization and the industry." Do not be lulled into a false sense of comfort when you are encouraged to pursue an employer with jobs available in your field of expertise, in spite of the fact that you have no work experience in that industry.

First, be sure you know what industry the organization is in. Second, know where the organization you are meeting with stands in relation to its competition. With the Internet and various search engines, obtain the information you need to be knowledgeable about the organization. Review your research. Are there any questions that you would like answered when you consider the organization's current financial condition? Where does it derive the major portion of its revenue? What is the product/service that provides the biggest profit margin? What about its parent? Be sure you know by name the various organizational entities associated with the organization with whom you are meeting, as well as how to correctly pronounce them.

Practice saying the names out loud so that you hear how they sound to your ears when you are saying them.

The more knowledgeable you become about the organization, the more confident and enthusiastic you will become. And that excitement will add to the timbre of your voice throughout the interview. On the other hand, the less you know, the more likely the opposite effect will occur with accompanying deflationary results that include some apprehension that you will sooner or later be asked something about the organization and its products/services/reputation that you are not be prepared to answer.

Answers to Demonstrate Your Reasons for Leaving Your Current and Past Employers

As we stated above when discussing disclosure and control, be sure to emphasize positive reasons or at least neutral reasons for leaving your present and past employers to the extent you are able to do so truthfully.

Neutral reasons are those having to do with the business problems the organization is having or had. These include:

> I really had no choice in leaving because the organization was sold and the acquiring organization already had a controller.

Or:

> The staff was reduced from 800 to 127 in just three months, and more layoffs were announced just before I contacted you.

Positive reasons are those that you present as opportunities.

> The company gave me the option to relocate, but it seemed to me at the time that there will be more career opportunities if I stay at this location.

Or:

> I wasn't looking for a job, but a recruiter kept calling and insisting that I just spend a few minutes with ABC Corporation because they were so interested in meeting with me.

Answers to Demonstrate Your Understanding of Your Strengths and Weaknesses

The strengths you identify should be impressive to the interviewer. To prepare, identify strengths that will help to make you successful in the position for which you are being considered.

"I am a team player," as an identification of strength is okay, but you can make a much more effective response. Try to identify a situation with a brief engaging story that exemplifies how you were able to solidify the team where you currently work.

> At XYZ Corporation we had serious problems with turnover on the team I was assigned to. Our numbers were the worst in the division. I suggested a new approach to the supervisor that I thought would solve this problem. I suggested that the team be given more autonomy in the completion of our daily tasks. We could try it for two weeks, and if production continued to be a problem, then she could try something else.
>
> Then I called the team members together and let them know we were going to take responsibility for our own production schedules. I reminded a few of the longer service members of the outside commitments that they wanted to be present for. I told them if the assignments were completed on a daily basis, the others would fill in so that they could attend the events they really wanted to. I then spoke to the remaining staff members and told them about these requests and reminded them that when they needed time off, the same courtesy would be extended.
>
> Day by day, the supervisor was impressed that the results were improving slightly. With more time, the team became so cohesive that some of the employees began to purchase lottery tickets together and bring in special lunches. The result is that turnover is down and productivity is up. Now we even have visitors from corporate headquarters who want to see what is going on and to determine whether what we are doing can be replicated elsewhere. I felt especially good the other day when one of the team members told me that he really looks forward to going to work now and before the changes, he was ready to quit. It seems that with the problems you are having on the line here, there might be an opportunity to try something similar.

As you can see in this example, the interviewer learns:

• What the problem was

- What you decided to do
- The outcome

Discussing weaknesses, on the other hand, can be difficult. Here you need to identify a weakness that is not really a weakness, such as:

- "I like an exceptionally clean desk."
- "I am a perfectionist."
- "I get so frustrated when others don't aim for the high quality of output that I seek."

Who will not think, "Wow, that's a weakness?" Be sure, though, to be ready to describe what you do to deal with it. Follow the above with: "I am realistic. I know that others have other priorities, so I try from their first day of employment to set the right professional tone and let them know they should expect no less."

If you say: "I can't say no." Be sure to follow with: "In my efforts to please and be of service, I try to be helpful to everyone, even if I already have a full plate. I have learned, though, that I am not alone, so when the demands are growing faster than I can handle them, I meet with my boss to be sure she is aware of the demands on my time and also to see if she has suggestions for completing all of these assignments."

Or if you say: "I am married to my work," continue by saying, "I suppose I should get a life outside work, but I really enjoy my work. Even though others might think I am shortchanging myself, I do not. To ensure that I am not becoming too one-sided, I discuss the issue periodically with my boss."

And don't forget to get them to ask you questions that will provide them with the information you want them to know before you leave the meeting.

How can you get interviewers to ask questions that allow you to introduce the answers you want them to know? The easiest way to do this is when you are given the opportunity to raise a question, "Do you have any questions?" In these situations take the tag line and raise it as a statement at the beginning of your question. For example, "When demands exceed the resources required to do the job where I am now working, I meet right away with my boss to be sure he is aware that a problem is looming and to outline steps to elimi-nate it before it becomes a serious problem. How do you deal with similar situations here?"

Two More Questions You Hope They Don't Ask: "What Are You Making?" or, "What Are You Looking For?"

The longer you can delay any discussion of pay, the better your position will be when this topic is raised. For starters, if they give you an application to complete, on it will be a request for pay data. You have a decision to make—include it or leave it blank and see if they catch it. If and when they do, just apologize for the omission. If they do not notice, then you are gaining additional time until they ask. There is usually a second area on the form that requests position you seek and desired salary. Here you should never include a figure or even a range but insert the word "open" or "flexible." You need to recall, though, what you put on the appli-cation when the topic comes up with interviewers. There might be some flexibility in putting a current pay amount. If you think you are underpaid, consider inserting a "total compensation" number that includes any bonus or benefits you receive. If you are thinking the offer will be a low one and you do not want to be eliminated, only give your base pay number—without the extras including bonus and stock options that you included in the total comp fig-ure. Never lie because you might be asked to provide a recent pay statement or some other form of proof.

If the topic comes up and you have yet to complete an appli-cation, avoid appearing evasive while also trying to delay sharing your data. Say something like: "I am moving primarily for a real career opportunity and money is not my primary focus, but what does this position pay?" "If the response is evasive, "We don't know yet because it is a new position." Then you might ask, "What has been budgeted?" If you are still being questioned about your pay at that point, you might qualify your answer, "My current rate of pay is X, but the position we are discussing here is quite different in nature and scope from my current level of responsibility." That should move the conversation away from the pay rate to the job description. Do not be dragged into any negotiation at this point. "What would you accept?" is one example that tries to draw you in. If raised, then say, "I really feel it is premature at this point to be discussing salary. I suggest we leave it until we reach agreement on other matters directly related to the open position first."

There is no substitution for preparation when you go to interview for a job. The best preparation is to be ready to discuss information about you that you have recently reviewed. It will make your answers crisp, clear, and well informed. As a result, you will accomplish your goal of either being invited back or offered the job. Either way it is a worthwhile objective to shoot for. (See Figure 10-2.)

Last-Minute Checklist

Key Points to remember when preparing answers

☐ Tell brief yet engaging stories

☐ Be ready with a two-minute (or less) summary to the "Tell me about yourself" question.

☐ Identify two key skills/talents/experiences that you will include in your answers as proof that you will do a great job, if hired.

☐ When giving accomplishment examples, restate them in this format:

— State the problem.

— Briefly tell what you did to address the problem.

— Provide the results, with numbers, wherever possible.

☐ Remember the principle of disclosure: share only when you need to—preferably when you want to.

☐ Remember the principle of control: the interviewer controls the interview; the applicant controls the flow of information—share only what you need to when responding to questions.

☐ Think positive. Great day. Great trip. Great interview. You currently have a great job, but this one is even better. In the past, always worked for great employers and terrific supervisors.

☐ When answering every question, always remember your objective. You need to demonstrate to the interviewer that:

— You *can do* the job (possess the skills);

— You *will do* the job (have the motivation;), and

— You will be a great *fit* (great to have around every day).

☐ Be ready with answers for :

"What do you know about us?"

"What are your strengths and weaknesses?"

"What are you currently making?"

"Why do you want to leave your current job?"

Figure 10-2

CHAPTER ELEVEN

Handling Difficult Questions

Whether you have 24 hours or days or even weeks to prepare for an interview, there is no excuse for not being fully prepared to handle difficult questions. The reason is threefold:

1. It will increase your readiness to address all and any questions. It is better to be prepared for difficult questions even if they are not asked. If you are ready for the tough ones that don't get asked, your readiness for the questions that should be "lay-ups" will hopefully put you on alert and give you an edge that you might otherwise not have. Just consider how you will feel if you blow any question —especially one that you consider was a gimme.

2. Preparing for your interview in a variety of ways gives you one more opportunity to prepare an overall presentation that is as sharp as it can be. The effect will be an even more impressive and confident you.

3. As a reminder to always stay alert — regardless the degree of apparent softness to any questions—consider all questions difficult.

Below we take you through a very practical approach to answering difficult questions. Following this approach will help you always be prepared for any question that might arise during the interview.

Questions You Hope They Do Not Ask

Questions you hope they do not ask can range from those that rattle the skeletons in your closet to the questions that you just do not know how to form the right answer to.

At the top of this list should be: "Tell me about yourself." We already discussed this sticky question in Chapter 10, but it is an important query, so we see fit to mention it again here. The positive side is that preparing for this question allows you to be ready with a summary statement that hopefully should open a dialogue, especially if you end your statement with, "... That is a brief overview. What part of my background would you like me now to expand?" Again, keep it brief and positive.

What Are Your "Sore" Spots? Where Do You Feel Vulnerable?

Determine what in your background/experience you prefer not to discuss. It might be that your resume does not provide a complete history of your professional life because you are concerned that if you added dates, you would be eliminated due to age discrimination. Or it might be that early in your career you made a major job change that led to a career switch, so you prefer not even to bring any employer's attention to that time in your life.

Why Questions

Do not become defensive with *why* questions, even though they might set a tone that puts you on the defensive. Examples of *why* questions include the following:

Why Are You Looking for a Job Now?   The implication is that you are doing something that you shouldn't. As with all the questions below, make sure to remember that your tone as well as the content of your answer is important. Your response will either convey a sense of *why did she have to ask that question* or *I am so glad that you asked.*

> Rather than delay putting my search off any longer, as busy as things are for me at work, I need to make the time to find my next career opportunity now—even though the market is weak and my obligations are time-consuming right now.

Why Did You Leave Your Last Employer/Why Do You Want to Leave Your Current Job?   Interviewers who are more astute will either ask, "Please share with me the circumstances surrounding your departure from XXX Corporation." Or they will wait you out so you will volunteer the answer before they have to raise the question themselves. However, many interviewers realize that you will share just as much—or more—if they are adept at framing the question more diplomatically. Regardless of how or when they ask (or wait without asking), this is a difficult question that you should handle in an effective manner that allows you to close this line of inquiry quickly. If you are successful, you will astutely move the interviewer onto a path of questions that is more positive in nature. Keep in mind, though, that whatever your answer to this question, you are not going to be offered a job. On the other hand, a negative or weak reply might knock you out of the running. Just to clarify, consider your response to the question as either a knockout or the opportunity to get to the next round. You need to remember that the question is raised and the answer sought not so much to convince the interviewer that you are the best candidate for the job under consideration, but rather for him to determine whether this discussion should be allowed to continue based on your answer. (To put it simply, the question is raised to determine whether there is a problem employee in the making here.)

The following is an example of an effective way to deal with this question:

> I was giving XYZ organization my all and had lost a lot of nights and weekends doing it. I did not mind at all because the work was really challenging and they were counting on me during a most trying time. I learned a lot, not only about the work, but also about who I am and what is important to me. I also realized that the more I did, the more I would be called upon to do, and sooner or later their increasing demands with insufficient resources would lead them to be dissatisfied with me. Putting all this together, I thought the best thing to do was to start looking around for my next opportunity. I could not do it and continue working at the same time, so I decided to address the topic. I wanted to give the organization its due and think well of me, so without another job in hand, I quit to devote my full-time energies and attention to my next career move, and here I am.

Here is another and more frequent variation:

> My position along with several others was eliminated as part of a major restructuring.

A good short, to-the-point response that includes the implicit understanding that this was nothing personal. You were swept up in a big layoff that left you no alternative.

In the process of answering, always be sure to avoid an emotional response, such as in the following:

> I was fed up and know I should not have, but I walked out because I could not take it anymore.

Or:

I got tired of being shoved around by one boss after another who had no idea of what to do.

These are statements that beg for elaboration—if, that is, the interviewer is not saying "end of interview" to herself. The more you try to elaborate, the more the interviewer is going to go through an encircling pattern of disbelief. Don't air dirty laundry, even if every word you say is 100-percent true.

Why Did You Decide to Go to (Name of School)?   Even if you just graduated, the question has no relevance to the job you are applying for. Do not, though, show any signs of impatience or worse.

It is a great school with a great reputation in (your major). Or, I did not have a lot of choice because it was close by and I had family obligations that would allow me to do both.

Be observant for any feedback clues being offered by the interviewer: "I ask because I went to (its archrival)." Try to be ready with a stock reply that addresses the perhaps unheralded reputation of the school, its program, and or its faculty.

Why Did You Decide to Major in (Name of Major)?   Again, there might be a hidden agenda or bias relating to the interviewer or the job under consideration. Regardless, take the high road. Be succinct.

It was a tough major and I wanted to prove to myself I could succeed.

Do not get involved with stories about the great teacher who influenced you so much that you thought that was the direction to pursue. Watch out too for the interviewer who is considering the school for his child. You are not there to provide counseling. Get to the topic at hand—the job that you need to show you are quite able to fill.

What Are Your Weaknesses?   This question is always a dangerous one because if you share a weakness that knocks you out of consideration, you did it to yourself. The key is to take a weakness that will be perceived as strength.

I never say no. As a person sensitive to customer service, I feel it is not right to say no to a request even if that request is made five minutes before quitting time. I might be setting the wrong example for those making the request, but I feel that the alternative is not acceptable. How do you feel about this?

It is also helpful and shows both insight and action to take a real weakness (not an overwhelming one) and show how you are taming it.

I really like to have a clean desk before I leave. As I have moved up the chain of command, I still prefer to start the day with a clean desk. Although it is not always possible, I try to do it as frequently as I can. The result is that I have learned to realize that not everything can be resolved in one day (especially if the issue arose toward the end of the day), yet by being flexible and still keeping that goal in mind, I have become more reasonable and effective as well.

What Has Been Your Greatest Failure? This is an opportunity to tell a story that shows what happened, why it was important, and what you learned or accomplished.

There was this administrative assistant who was a terrific performer until he started to have personal problems. Once I noticed his performance start to deteriorate, I met with him and he shared with me the problems he was having in his personal life. I encouraged him to contact the EAP, and I reminded him that I considered him a key contributor to our team's goals. I asked if in some way I could be of additional assistance. He said he appreciated my offer and my concern. I told him we should meet on a weekly basis to discuss ways in which his performance could improve, and he could bring me up to date on the resolution of his personal problem. He agreed and thanked me for my support. Unfortunately, in spite of the weekly meetings, his performance continued to deteriorate. I kept Human Resources informed and eventually he was fired. This has been my greatest failure because I was not able to prevent him from being fired in spite of the potential he displayed. This was the first time I realized that even great employees cannot always become winners.

Be ready also for this variation to the greatest failure question: "Describe a situation where you were not able to convince others to accept your proposal." Try to identify a situation where you initially failed but ultimately were successful. Your persistence and problem-solving ability will both stand out and hold you in good stead with the interviewer.

> I had found a sales opportunity that would have meant my total goal for the quarter. My boss was impressed, as was the CEO. We were all ready to finalize the terms, but the CFO would not give his approval. He was concerned about their credit rating. The problem was not a bad payment history, but a recent record of very slow payments. Without the CFO's blessing, the CEO and my boss would not let the deal go through. I was quite frank with my customer and stayed in touch with them. At the same time I began to periodically run reference checks. When they showed signs of improvement in their payment history, I checked internally to see if I could influence opinions to change. Once I did, I then returned to the customer with a preapproved offer.

What Areas Have Been Problems in Other Interviews?   As part of your preparation, recall any questions that presented challenges (not problems) in previous interviews. Going forward, be sure to jot them down as part of your debriefing after the interview. Review what made them difficult, and practice answers in front of a colleague or spouse. This practice will not only determine how they sound to you but also will allow you to gain insight from the person hearing them.

Honestly Confront Problems Yourself

Regardless of the degree of difficulty in any question, there is never a reason to lie during the interviewing process for two big reasons:

- First, when you tell one person a lie, then you have to remember whom you told it to and what specifically you said. That gets complicated fast.
- Second, once you have lied about something in your background, you will always wonder if and when it will be discovered. Finding a job is tough enough without having a dark cloud always following you around.

Tell the facts, get past it, and get on with the interview when you do have to own up to some past errors. If they say:

I see that you checked off the box that states you have been convicted of a felony.

Be truthful and answer:

Yes, it is true and I will always be ashamed that I have to check off that box whenever asked, but let me say it was a really dumb mistake that I made as a teenager. I paid a hefty price for what I did, and I have wised up since.

Then be quiet and see what feedback you are given.

Remember, this is public information and best to disclose it up front, if asked, and remember to share only what you need to.

Questions You Know They Should Not Ask

Interviewers continue to skirt the law by asking questions that are either borderline or downright illegal. More often than not, the person making the error is doing so because he is an inexperienced and poorly trained interviewer. You certainly are entitled under the law to file a complaint if the question is protected by law, but to do so requires a time commitment that might best be put to use looking for jobs elsewhere.

Illegal Areas

Federal, state, and local laws prohibit employment discrimination based on certain criteria. The easiest way for an employer to avoid having discrimination claims filed against it is to avoid raising these issues in an interview. It is not the mere asking of an illegal question that is the problem; it is the discrimination in offering—or denying— a job based on the response (or nonresponse) to one of these questions. So the smart interviewers steer clear of them. (See Figure 11-1.)

Borderline Areas

There is another category of questions, BFOQ's, that are okay to ask if there is a job-related reason to do so. If there isn't, then they should not be asked.

- BFOQ's—in those situations that require a Bona Fide Occupational Qualification. For example, "Do you speak

Illegal Question Topics

Race
Color
National origin
Religion
Gender
Pregnancy
Age (a protected category for those 40 and over)
Disability
Vietnam era veteran
Disabled veteran
Arrest record
Any garnishment
Bankruptcy
Filing of a workers' compensation claim

Figure 11-1

Spanish?" is a valid question if you are seeking a position in a hospital where your position would require you to speak Spanish because a majority of patients that you would meet speak only Spanish. If you seek a position that requires some modeling and the organization only makes women's clothes, they will be allowed to hire only women for that position.

Illegal Questions and When You Might Want to Answer

If you are woman interviewing for a position with heavy overtime, the interviewer is on dangerous grounds if she asks, "Do you have children?" The point is that the interviewer in her bumbling way, more likely than not, is only trying to determine if you will be available to handle the heavy overtime. A more appropriate way to ask the question would be for the interviewer to state for both male and female candidates, "This position will require frequent and sometimes last-minute overtime demands. Will you be able to meet these requirements?"

Here is an opportunity for you to disclose what neither men nor women need to: "I have two teenagers at home, and I have very responsible arrangements to ensure that they are provided for when I need to stay late at work. This has not been a problem for me in the past, and I am certain it will not be a problem for me if you offer me this position." (See Figure 11-2.)

Last-Minute Checklist

Interview Reminders

☐ Never be afraid to say: *"I don't know"* or *"Nothing comes to mind at the moment."* Agree to provide the information later, in a phone call or letter.

☐ Don't whine. All those problems with your job, your life, or the job search brings too many negatives into the interview.

☐ Remember the *"we's."* You did not do it all yourself. Do not make it all about *"I did this or that."*

☐ Do not take conversation into illegal areas by accident. Control disclosure.

☐ Hold onto your professional outlook even if you are asked illegal or inappropriate questions.

☐ Questions are illegal if asked orally or on an application form before you are offered a job. Afterwards, it is acceptable to inquire about health, gender, age, and marital status for insurance and EEOC reports.

☐ If you feel you have been discriminated against, contact your local Equal Employment Opportunity Office.

Figure 11-2

CHAPTER TWELVE

Ten Crucial Last-Minute Checks

As interview time approaches, you need to be properly and wisely prepared. No staying up for an "all-nighter." No cramming. Although your interview is certainly a test, it is not a school test. It will be an opportunity for you to show what you know and what you have done. You have already sold yourself to the organization through your resume, and now they wish to meet with you for an interview.

They want to learn more about you; they want to see who this person is who looked so much like a winner and must-hire on paper. You have enticed them with your initial paperwork and contact so that they want to learn more. They are inviting you in to meet so that they can confirm what they have already seen from your resume. Celebrate the fact that you received an invitation to meet. Be sure you do not take the meeting for granted, but also do not feel guilty if you could not do more preparation. Wisely use the time you have to get ready, but do not be concerned with the *"If I only had..."* regrets.

If you have not read the other chapters, in an attempt to conserve time, you should consult *this chapter* before the interview. As you go through the 10 points, if one of them causes a sinking feeling of *"oh...I never thought of that"* or *"I am not prepared for that,"* then go to the appropriate chapter and get up to speed. Do not squander this interview. They are too hard to come by!

Even if you are being interviewed as a courtesy due to a contact, remember that there were specific reasons the company agreed to this meeting. So even in these circumstances when there might be less reason to be optimistic about the identification of a specific job, you will be wise to assume that if they like you they will find an opportunity for you to join them —if not immediately, then perhaps sometime in the future. In other words, you never know what impact you will have on people or organizations. (See Figure 12-1.)

Five Checkpoints to Address Before You Depart for the Interview

1. Be Comfortable. You Should Feel Like a Winner.

Look inside yourself to determine your comfort and confidence levels. The opportunity should be one in which you have a chance to shine. Are you approaching it in that way? Are you listening to

---

Checklist before You Leave for Interview

✓ Mirror check

✓ Sales pitch

✓ Why should they hire you?

✓ Why do you want to work there?

✓ Accessories: resume, ID card

Figure 12-1

negative voices warning you that you need this job because you are financially strapped and there is no other opportunity on the table right now? If this feeling is surfacing, recognize it and then consider what you have control over and what you don't.

Remind yourself that you are totally ready for this meeting because you have done your preparation and you have very good examples of your work to discuss. You realize that the meeting might not lead to a job, but you also know that it might. Remember that not only are you prepared, but also that they would be lucky to have you because of what you bring to the table and what you perceive to be their challenges at this time. Once you reaffirm your inner self, remind yourself that there is only so much you can control during this meeting. Let go of the *"what ifs?"*

Once that is done and you are confirming the positive aspects of what you have to offer, it is time then to look at your outer self and perform a "puff and buff check." How do you look? Face and hair check? Shoes polished? Nails trimmed? Appropriate outfit? Keep any pockets relatively empty—no need to bring all your change, keys, credit cards, and pens. Look for clean, trim lines — avoid the baggy look even if you are interviewing for a position with one of Universal Music's hip-hop labels.

Are you dressed appropriately? Your look should convey the following impressions: neat, professional, stylish, contemporary, serious (with a touch of very light humor only if you insist). Lay out your outfit the night before your interview so that regardless of what takes place in the morning, you do not have to be concerned that the blue suit you were planning to wear is still in the cleaners or that it is missing one or more buttons. By making these wardrobe decisions in advance, you not only can eliminate any last minute problems but also any opportunity to have doubts of your own ability to be prepared. You also give yourself more time and the confidence to focus on other things.

2. Thirty-Second Sales Pitch

The "tell me about yourself" question is an opportunity to do your own infomercial. You have already prepared yourself for this question, but you need to review by rehearsing to ensure that your sales pitch is:

- Fresh and vital in your mind
- Brief and relevant for the position for which you are being considered.

3. Why Should They Hire You?

If you cannot tell them, who will? This is the core reason for the interview: What points do you want to be sure to make? What message about yourself do you want to leave with the interviewer? You know you will be asked this question in some form or another; if not, then you must be certain to tell them precisely why they should offer you the job.

Review what makes you unique and what is it about you that will help to separate you from all the other candidates, both internal and external.

> With my specific expertise and recent training in knowledge management, I will quickly be able to assist each of the IT team members currently working on the project and increase their skill to a "best practice" level so that the organization might then consider what is most applicable in this environment.

4. Why You Want to Work There

Be careful here. Be wary about thinking solely in terms of the organization. You also need to include the specific unit in which the position you are being considered for is located, as well as the team and supervisor. You need to be careful that your information and impressions are accurate, current, and appropriate. At the same time, be sure that you address the situation in positive terms. (For example, you don't see difficulties but rather challenges.) Actually, this is superb preparation just before the meeting because you will, by preparing here, be reviewing the opportunity to confirm that it is as good as you earlier thought it was. Recall, too, the reasons you initially applied to the organization and for this specific position. Based on what you have learned since, what is it about the position that makes you really want it—now more than ever?

The interviewer will want to hear not just your interest in joining the organization, but also what makes this position so appealing to you. Is this a form of flattery? Absolutely, but it also is a very direct signal from you that you are aware and astute organizationally because you realize that positions—especially in this highly competitive and global marketplace—don't just become available. They are sought and approved only when there is a real need in meeting organizational demands by filling this position.

If you have the time, take a last skim through online sources and/or the papers to see if there are any last-minute developments that directly or indirectly impact the organization that you are meeting with. If the organization is publicly traded, should they be coming out with quarterly numbers? If so, plan to get them. If there are any public announcements related to those numbers, see what the company says those numbers reflect and what their business prospects are going forward. See too if there were any last-minute merger or acquisition announcements.

By keeping abreast of any last-minute headlines, you will be in a position to ask: "What impact will the newest development have on this organization and/or the position that we are discussing today?" That will also highlight your interest and business acumen. Remember that you are also interviewing them. A key point is that this latest information might very well affect your desire to work there at all.

5. Materials

Just as we warned about being careful not to overprepare mentally, plan also to be judicious in determining what physical items you want to bring. We are talking about the essential materials—at least two copies of your resume, your business card, directions, and the name, title, and phone number of both the person with whom you are to meet and the person (if different) who arranged the meeting.

Take only what you need. The less you have, the less likely you are to fumble and the more organized you will appear. If you have a leather portfolio or binder, that is fine. If not, consider purchasing plain file folders that you can take to hold copies of your resume and the other information pertaining to this specific meeting. If you have research materials, keep them separate and, depending on whether you are driving or not, consider whether you need to bring them with you. You probably will be better off leaving all of it in the car.

If you are driving, you have much greater latitude concerning what you need to bring. You could bring whatever you want and just leave everything in the car except for the folder with your resume and contact information of the person with whom you are meeting. If you are driving, you can bring the paper, research that you have gathered, comments, and notes from earlier conversations—all of which you can review to remind you what you learned earlier.

Since 9/11 there are various security precautions to enter buildings and garages that might impact on your arrival time. Remember to ask when you confirm your appointment if there are building security precautions that might delay your arrival; some buildings require that a messenger from the organization escort all visitors to their offices, for example. Always have a picture ID just in case.

Five Checkpoints for "At the Interview" Site: 15 Minutes before

You are on site—either sitting in your car or in a lobby, waiting to go to your appointment so that you plan your arrival no earlier than 15 minutes before your scheduled appointment. While you are waiting, use the time wisely. (See Figure 12-2.)

1. Energy/Adrenaline/Passion

You need to get pumped up and excited. Doing so will give you an edge and additional energy. If you arrive too early to go into the building, determine what to do. If it is just for a few minutes, look for a bench, assuming it is a nice day. If longer, try a local fast food

---

Checklist When You Arrive for Interview

✓ Energy levels
✓ Appearance
✓ Points to make
✓ Relaxed but alert
✓ Manners

Figure 12-2

outlet where you can review the material you brought, including a quick scan of today's paper for any last minute breaking news affecting the organization with whom you are meeting. During this time though, get your adrenalin flowing. Do not be lulled into a state of serenity watching the clouds roll by. Stay focused on your meeting ahead, and review any items you wish to see one more time. Remember why you are there. When you park the car, walk briskly into the building so that you get the blood flowing.

When you arrive in the office 15 minutes before your scheduled appointment, greet the receptionist with a friendly and energetic *"Good morning/Good afternoon/Good day"* loud enough to be sure he can hear you but careful not to shout.

2. Appearance

When you arrive in the reception area at least 15 minutes before your scheduled time, visit the rest room to do a last-minute check on your appearance. Making sure that your commute or stop over for coffee has left nothing amiss or any reminders of muffin lingering around your mouth, this is also a good chance to release any stress. Deep breaths and you are ready!

3. Points to Make

First, review the major points you want this company to be sure they hear from you. Second, take a moment to consider what questions you had regarding the job and the organization. Have some questions ready because at some point the interviewer will ask, *"I have been asking all the questions to this point, now let me be sure I am giving you the time to ask yours."* You might have some questions due to the interviewer's information. However, just in case the interviewer has not raised any issues that warrant a question from you, it is essential that you have at least one relevant question to ask so that you do not have to give the weak response: *"No. I am fine."*

Regarding small talk, take your lead from the interviewer and don't linger. No big deal here. Just be ready with a quick, light comment regardless of the question. Be positive, friendly, and brief. You want to get away from small talk and start focusing on to the substance of the meeting.

Remember the rules of disclosure. Do not present yourself as a potential stalker. Avoid demonstrating your Internet prowess by letting your interviewer know the high school she attended or the last time she ran the marathon.

4. Relaxed but Not Too Comfortable

Remind yourself to relax, but do not confuse that with being comfortable. When you are relaxed, you are in control of your words and your actions. You are a good listener because you are not overwhelmed. You feel quite pleased with yourself in this situation and sense that you are able to listen carefully. If you are too comfortable, you will lose the edge that keeps you sharp, and you also run the danger of allowing the interviewer to get you to lower your guard. Don't forget that the best interviewers are the ones that get you to feel very much at ease (that is, comfortable) so that they will be able to extract more information from you when your guard is lowered. (*"*You are such a nice person and I probably shouldn't be telling you this, but…")

5. Manners

Finally don't forget that you need to be polite and good mannered to all throughout your interview. This attitude for success should start even before you arrive at the building. That, by the way, is another reason to be conservative about the travel time you need. When we are late, we try to cut corners—run in front of slow-moving pedestrians, make a U-turn in a double-line zone because we just missed our turn, or cut off a person as we head into the parking lot. These are all inexcusable acts that might reduce, and even eliminate, your chances if anyone connected to the interview process was a witness to your actions.

That's it. Consider yourself prepared and get ready to begin the interview. (See Figure 12-3.)

Last-Minute Checklist

Top Reasons Candidates "Fail" Interviews

Lateness	Tactlessness
Passiveness	Lack of eye contact
Too interested in money	Evasive responses
Poor references	Inflexible expectations
Arrogance	Lack of interest in company
Overstated qualifications	Poor appearance
Lack of preparation	Looked different on paper
Immaturity	Lack of attentiveness
Strong biases	Nervousness
Poor speaking skills	Sloppy appearance
Preoccupied with benefits	Poor manners
Sloppy application form	Unwilling to give references

Resume differs from application details

...and just a feeling or general impression "I don't know why. "

Figure 12-3

Follow-Up

CHAPTER THIRTEEN

Assess Your Performance and Evaluate the Company

The side benefit of interviews is that the more you do, the better you get at it. The more comfortable you become in an interview, the more experienced you become in dealing with different types of interviewers, and the more successful you will be in your interview!

What Did You Do Right?

Mentally replay the interview—from greeting to closing. Did you feel energetic and psyched up for the interview? Were you confident that you were prepared and ready to present yourself as an excellent candidate? Were you comfortable in your dress and grooming? Did you feel that you "fit" in and were appropriately attired?

Go back to the three goals you established in Chapter 7. Did you get your message across to the interviewer? Did you ask questions and get the information that you needed?

Give yourself a pat on the back and mark down everything that went right. This step helps boost your confidence and gives you a list to remember for your next interview. (See Figure 13-1.)

What Did They Do Right?

If the interviewer is rating your candidacy, you should also review his performance.

Overall, was the organization how you expected it to be? From your research you formed a mental image of the company—how did it match in reality? Did it compare favorably to other similar organizations you have visited?

As we've stated previously, it is very easy to be myopic in the interview process and forget that you are also considering them as a possible employer. Granted, in a tight job market, these considerations might weigh less heavily, but it is still wise to assess the employer for both viability as well as to determine how it would feel to be an employee at that company. As long as you realize that a job might not be "the right one" but the one "right now," there is nothing wrong in accepting a position that is a stepping-stone to another in the future if you are willing to do a day's work for a day's wage. Employers no longer promise employment for life, nor do they expect unlimited loyalty from their employees.

What I Did Right

Mentally go through interview from beginning to end.
What were the things you did right?

- **Preparation**

  Research about organization, industry, job was sufficient.

- **Greeting/Small Talk**

  Did you feel comfortable?

- **Setting the Parameter**

  Did you restate why you were there, the purpose of the interview? Were you able to establish rapport with interviewer?

- **The Main Event**

  Did you feel you were prepared for questions? Were you able to answer questions as you had planned? Did you get your message across?

- **Your turn**

  Did you get the information you needed about the organization and/or the job? Did you ask the questions you planned to ask?

- **Closing**

  Did you learn what their next step will be? Did you indicate any action to be taken on your part?

Figure 13-1

Having a realistic appraisal of an organization is essential to determining if you want to be employed there for any length of time. To ignore certain signs, such as a poor attitude towards employees or not having funds to make needed plant repairs, can make your effort futile. You cannot have a crystal ball to predict whether the company will stay in business or be profitable in the long run, but you certainly do not want to be the last employee hired at the next Enron! (See Figure 13-2.)

What Could You Have Done Better?

Every interview could have gone better. You can only control your side of the equation. There are many variables that are totally out of your sphere of influence such as *"Did the interviewer have a good commute to work that morning?"* or *"How long has she been working as an interviewer?"* But you can control what you say and do, and how you perform in an interview—and you can improve that performance.

If you could do the entire interview over again, what would you do differently? What could you have done to improve the entire experience? List five things that you could have done better or differently, and why these are important. (See Figure 13-3.)

Assessing the Interviewer

Start on time?

Prepared?

    Had read your resume ahead of time?

    Knowledge of job opening?

    Knowledge of organization?

    Knowledge of industry/economy?

Personal chemistry...rapport established with you?

Attentive?

    Good listener?

    Follow-up comments or questions?

Gave clear understanding of what next steps would be?

Gave impression actively interested in your candidacy?

Figure 13-2

If I could do the interview over differently, I would:	Because:
1	
2	
3	
4	
5	

Figure 13-3

What Could They Have Done Better?

Considering that this organization is seeking to attract new and qualified employees, their performance also should have been top notch—from the reception area to the interviewer.

Was the interviewer prepared; were you expected? Did he have your resume? Did you have a private area to talk?

What might you infer from the treatment you received? If the interviewer lacked knowledge of the organization and/or the job opening, what importance does the company place on this position? If the interviewer was ill-mannered or lacking in social skills, what type of company would hire someone like that to represent them in the marketplace?

Record your impressions of both the interviewer and the organization gleaned from the interview itself. Should a job offer be forthcoming, it is important to revisit these observations. It is easy, in the glow of a job offer, to forget or gloss over negative points only to regret them later. (See Figure 13-4.)

Where Might You Have Been Better Prepared? Any Surprise Questions?

Even if you had unlimited time to prepare, you cannot imagine every single question that the interview might ask. How can you prepare for something like: "If you were on a merry-go-round, what color horse would you choose to ride?"

There are various topics open to discussion in an interview; when did you feel you gave the weakest answers? Why do you feel that way?

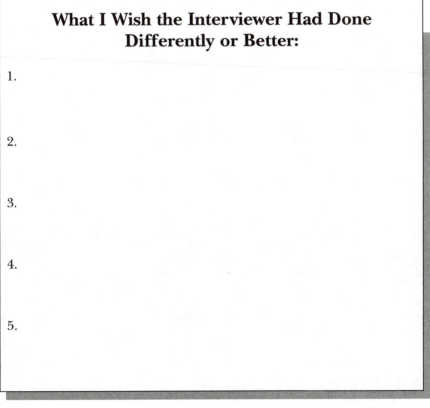

What I Wish the Interviewer Had Done Differently or Better:

1.

2.

3.

4.

5.

Figure 13-4

What questions totally surprised you? Now, with hindsight, what answers do you wish you had come up with? (See Figure 13-5.)

Putting It All into Perspective

You will have more interviews. You might get called back for further interviews with this same organization. You might get worse interviewers; you might get excellent interviewers. You might have more than 24 hours to prepare (hooray!).

What they asked:	How I wish I had answered:

Figure 13-5

What are five key points that you would write for yourself for your next interview? It can be as simple as never wearing those black shoes again to rewriting your resume or rethinking your prime job objective. One trait most companies treasure in an employee is the ability to learn from mistakes as well as to learn to avoid them! In this economy, we all must strive to be lifelong learners because change is all around us. (See Figure 13-6.)

How Does the Organization Stack up as a Possible Employer?

If you get a call back for a follow-up—presumably hiring—interview, will you feel anxious, relieved, or jubilant? What is your overall

---

My Personal "Never Forget" before an Interview Reminder List

1.

2.

3.

4.

5.

Figure 13-6

impression of this organization as a prospective employer? Can you really see yourself working for that company? Do you want the job as it has been portrayed to you?

It is so easy after an interview to have an afterglow—to remember all those good points and conveniently forget those troubling facts that you discovered in your research or in the interview yourself. Granted, all jobs are not created perfect; there are always adjustments to make. But it is important to be honest and realistic about your career moves. Do you still want the job *after* the interview as much as you did before? Or has it become less attractive? Most importantly, do you think they were impressed with your qualifications and skills? Do you think they will make you a job offer? (See Figure 13-7.)

Last-Minute Checklist

Remember why interviews are good for you

☐ Interviews help you understand what the employer needs.

☐ Interviews help you decide if you want the job.

☐ Interviews are the only way to communicate these "needs" and "wants."

Figure 13-7

CHAPTER FOURTEEN

Thank You's and Follow-Up

It is important that you keep your name (and your candidacy) in front of the interviewer and the organization after the interview. Although it is common courtesy to thank someone for their time and attention, many job seekers miss this valuable opportunity to restate the reasons why they are a great hire while impressing the interviewer with their social savvy.

Following Up versus Stalking

Sending someone an appropriate thank you is different from being in their face 24/7. Calling repeatedly, sending gifts or other reminders is not the way to show your confidence in being the right person for the job. The goal is to keep your positive attributes in the interviewer's mind—not to change her impression of you to one of a stalker.

What Action Was Cited in Your Close of the Interview?

How did the interview end? Did you learn what their time frame is for filling the position? What did you say when you exited the interview?

If you stated that you would contact the interviewer in a few days, do so but immediately. Send a thank-you note. Then, when you do call, you will have the advantage of having reminded her of your key selling points in advance.

> Hi, this is _____. I was in your office on ____ and interviewed for the position of _____. You indicated at the time that you hoped to fill the position by the end of this week. Have you made a decision?

Or:

> Oh, you are still considering other candidates? Is there any additional information that you need from me? Am I still being considered?

What if the interviewer was noncommittal about when the vacancy will be filled or put you off with a *"don't call us; we'll call you"* attitude? Still send a thank-you note, raise the issue in your closing asking when the job will be filled, and state that you will call at a specific moment (for example, in three days).

Thank You's

Using the words "thank you" is a very simple act that can mean the difference between being forgotten and being the candidate that keeps coming up on the interviewer's radar screen. Additionally, do not discount the value of keeping doors open. Even if the chances of getting the job are slim, other jobs with the organization might open up in the future. You never know when you might find yourself scheduling another interview with the same person.

Do not forget that, if hired, you will be part of the organization! Start off on the right foot—be gracious and be smart. If you have not written a business letter in some time other than your marketing/cover letter, pay attention to the form. (See Figure 14-1.)

When to Send?

Send immediately. If you have a morning interview, send it out that afternoon. Do not put it off. Refer to the notes you made after the interview for salient facts. Did you discuss any recent developments in the industry? If so, do you have an article that might interest her?

To Whom?

Send a separate thank you to every person you met with. If you were given their business cards, then the job is easy. If not, call their reception area and ask for the proper spelling and title of each person.

Was this a referral? Do not forget to send a note of appreciation to whoever set up the interview or recommended you. Let the recruiter know you are appreciative of his/her efforts and give an update. (See Figures 14-2 to 14-4.)

How to Send?

You can never be wrong in sending a *handwritten* thank you on your personal stationery. In this high-tech world, the effort to write something by hand is both noticed and appreciated by many in the business world. Use neat handwriting and professional-looking paper (leave the pictures of cats or sports scenes for other correspondence). If you prefer, type it first and then copy it if you are more comfortable working that way. If you don't like your penmanship, send the final version in typed format.

Business Letter Form

Use your Letterhead
Or formal note paper

Date

Name
Title
Organization
City, State Zip

Dear Mr./Ms./Mrs./Dr.:

Paragraph 1: Appreciation for specific time, date of interview for specific job.

Paragraph 2: Brief statement of why you want job/why suited for it.

Paragraph 3: Closing. State follow-up action.

Regards/Sincerely,

Signature

Figure 14-1

If you determine that the individuals and the organization march to a "time is money" beat and feel that the culture is more attuned to electronic correspondence, then send an e-mail to each person. Do not copy them on the same message! Each one should get their own. Many organizations have listings of key executives on their Web sites so that you can obtain their e-mail addresses.

Time is of the essence? They are making a decision in the next few days? Perhaps your thank you will arrive too late. In those cases, feel free to call to express your appreciation. Plan what you will say in advance, much like a written thank you, but

Sample Thank-You Letter for a Referral

Letterhead

January 12, 2004

Ms. Deidre Wallings
Senior Vice President-Operations
DFG Inc.
123 Main Street
Mentor, Ohio 44060

Dear Ms. Wallings,

Thank you so much for the information you gave me regarding the recent vacancy in the bookkeeping department at Winston & Evans, Ltd. This morning I had a very positive interview with Mr. Jameson in the Human Resources Department.

The job seems a great match, and the organization is very similar to the law firm where I had been employed at in Michigan.

I really appreciate your offering your time and advice to another fellow alumni of Marymount College. As my job search progresses, I will fill you in on further details at the next Alumni gathering.

With much appreciation,

Janice Greene Hastings

Figure 14-2

Sample Thank-You Letter for an Interview

Letterhead

January 10, 2004

Mr. Edward Stennings
Human Resources Director
CityTrust Bank
56 Crosswind Avenue
Jersey City, New Jersey 06903

Dear Mr. Stennings,

In our interview this afternoon regarding the position of Loan Officer, you gave me great insight into the markets CityTrust seeks to expand and its inner workings. The prospects for promoting consumer lending sounds challenging and creative—both of which are my strong suits.

As we discussed, my prior experience in consumer lending and particularly in credit card operations would be ideal for CityTrust. Additionally, my fluency in Spanish and Portuguese would be excellent tools for inroads into the inner-city market.

If there is any additional information I can provide, please do not hesitate to contact me. I will telephone you on January 24th to follow up on my application.

Thank you again for all your assistance.

Regards,

Hector Ezquela

Figure 14-3

Sample Thank-You Letter 2
for an Interview

Letterhead

January 15, 2004

Mrs. K. Rae Cane
Vice President Marketing
Oliver Enterprises
900 Broadway
New York, NY 10011

Dear Mrs. Cane,

I greatly appreciate your spending time with me this afternoon to discuss the internship program at Oliver Enterprises. It was particularly helpful to hear the academic requirements for those coveted positions.

When I return to school for my junior year, I will be registering for both Global Business and Marketing Statistics, as you recommended. Next year, at this time, I hope to apply again for the internship program with more appropriate credentials.

Again, I appreciate your candor and look forward to seeing you at the Career Fair this spring on campus.

Sincerely,

Joseph Thompson

Figure 14-4

please do not read it on the phone. Be natural, confident, and appreciative.

Corrective Measures/Address Weakness(es)

Remember when we asked what you thought you could have done better in the interview? What did you forget to mention?

A thank you is another opportunity to correct any faux pas made in the interview itself, such as:

> When you asked me about what new products I had developed, I neglected to mention the _____ , which is coming out this month. We had kept it under wraps for so long until the launch that it was ingrained in me not to talk about it.

Or:

> Since we were discussing my prior employment history, I overlooked my related volunteer activities. I mentor high school students who express an interest in science careers; I just started doing it this fall, and I am learning more than I am teaching!

Final Sales Pitch

Earlier in the book you listed your interview goals (see Chapter 7) as well as developed an answer to "Why should we hire you?" Now is the time to reevaluate those goals and restate your answer to that very important question.

Every interview is an opportunity for selling yourself. The organization seeks to find a solution to their problems, and you are selling yourself as the solution.

- What are the reasons that you want to work in that job for that organization? Remind them of your interest.

  The highlight of the interview was when we talked about product development. I have long admired your excellent line of products and your constant introduction of new ones that seem just right for the market and the time.

- Why are you perfect for this organization and this job? State your case again. Seeing it in print many times is a stronger statement than verbalizing it.

> With my experience in product development combined with your team-based approach, I am very excited at the prospect of working at _____. As I mentioned in the interview, teams were the essence of operational success at ____, my former employer. My familiarity with teams, both as a member and as a leader, gives me a valuable appreciation of the dynamics of teams.

Final Follow-Up Tasks

If you promised to send information or make a telephone call, remember to do so. Indicate on your postinterview notes what you did and when. What was the response of the interviewer, if any? Was she warm and receptive on the telephone? Is further action needed?

Should you be told that the position has already been filled—and not by you—do not burn your bridges. Many times new hires do not even show up for the first day of work, negotiations fall through on terms of employment, or they just do not work out; keep relations friendly.

> I am glad that you did find someone to fill the position—it is a vital part of your organization. Should another vacancy open up suited to my experience and skills, would you consider me for it? Feel free to contact me either by telephone or e-mail at any time. Your organization impresses me and I still would love to work there.

If the individual sounds interested, then be assertive:

> Let's keep in touch. I will call you in a month to see how things are going.

You might get put off, more of the "don't call us; we'll call you" vibe or even a bluntly honest "We really do not see a need for your experience/skills in our organization." You can press your luck and ask what there was about your work experience or interview that first caused them to invite you in but afterwards seemed to miss the mark. Just do not turn this into a confrontation; you are politely asking ways to improve your interviewing skills for the future and appreciate any comments that he can share. (See Figure 14-5.)

Last-Minute Checklist

Thank-You Reminders

☐ **Accuracy counts**. Proofread your thank-you letter for errors in spelling, punctuation.

☐ **Be presentable.** Investing in a nice letterhead or good paper will improve your presentation. A quality paper on the letterhead designed on your computer is another solution.

☐ **Be correct** in names, titles of addressees.

☐ **Be businesslike.** Either hand-write or computer address envelopes...please, no labels.

☐ **Be thorough.** Send letters to everyone associated with the interview.

☐ **Be sincere**. Express appreciation for the "extras"—time spent explaining the job, the organization, setting up further interviews.

☐ **Follow up.** If you say you will call, mark your calendar accordingly and do make the phone call.

Figure 14-5

CHAPTER FIFTEEN

Follow-Up Interviews

Act 2—You Made the First Cut

The waiting is over (well, at least until the next step, it is). You received a call telling you they want you to return to meet again. Take a moment to bask in the sweet success, then it's back to work to get ready for the next session(s).

First, you should feel terrific. Out of the hundreds of resumes they might have received, you were one of the few invited for a screening interview—that might even have only taken place after getting through a prescreening phone interview.

Consider too all the self-doubt that you addressed when deciding whether to apply for the job in the first place. As we said up front in Chapter 1, before one applicant completes a successful job search, he will have been seriously considered for at least 20 different jobs—if not 30—in most typical job searches.

Then, in spite of your fears and concerns about blowing the interview, you now know you did not. Congratulations are definitely in order.

Feel terrific for two reasons. The first you do not have any control over. Reason number one to feel terrific is because they are still trying to fill the position. Often these days we are told, "The position is on hold," or worse, "Due to careful review and most recent developments in _____, the position will not be filled at this time." There is still a very real opening, and you are being considered to fill it.

Feel terrific for a second reason as well. That is because of all the persons the organization has met with up until today, you are one who has passed the review from your first interviewer, the gatekeeper, and now are moving on to meet with one or more persons most probably in the department where the opening is actually located. In addition, you know what? Even if the first interviewer had some doubts, once you move past that "gatekeeper"—regardless of the level of excellence (or not) heaped upon you by her—you have moved past the gatekeeper (probably a staff member from Human Resources). Keep in mind that with each progressive step you take, it is becoming increasingly possible that eventually you will actually receive a job offer.

All that said, now is the time to research, rehearse, and relax.

Reprise. What Was Good about the First Interview? (Research—Part One)

Celebrate your victories and do not be condemned to your past mistakes. Look at your notes to determine what you did right at that first interview. Start at the very beginning. How was the trip? How hard was it to find the office once you arrived? How difficult was it to get past security? How friendly were they? Did you fill out an application (more on this below)? What was the climate/environment like? Did they keep you waiting? Should you bring something to read? Did you ask for an annual report? How long were you there?

- Review your interview notes from your previous meetings. Figure 15-1 will help jar your memory. Hopefully your notes are an accurate source of recall. The better you are at recalling what happened, the more you can attempt to determine whether the damage done was real or imagined, and hopefully it is an opportunity to boost your confidence. Remember they did invite you back and you are going. (See Figure 15-1.)

- What new points can you make? Pull out the original ad you responded to along with your reply. Check the date. How long did it take them to contact you? How long did it take to get a meeting? Were they flexible? Did they insist on meeting between nine and five? Were they respectful of your time? Is there anything that you need or want to bring to this next meeting? If the meeting was scheduled more than two days ago, do you want to call to confirm before the session is to occur? (There are some, especially among sales professionals, who would argue that you should not call out of fear they might cancel.)

- What should you be ready to discuss? Consider reviewing our earlier discussion on disclosure (see Chapter 10). It is good to recall the concept here because the stakes are getting higher and you want to determine (while being careful) what you want to disclose and when, while looking for additional disclosure from your interviewers as well. Consider the topics shown in Figure 15-2 to determine what you wish to

Review Your First Interview Notes. Consider the Following:

Whom did you meet with?

What was/were the person(s) title(s)? Business Unit/ Department Name?

What issues were raised?

Any concerns come to your mind?

Do you think they had any themselves?

What did you send after your meetings and to whom?

If there are any issues that were raised by you in any of your follow-up correspondence, was it addressed?

Did you send any additional information? Application? Articles?

What was it that you liked and didn't like about your first interview?

Describe the person(s) you met with?

What did they like about you?

What issues did they raise?

What did you like about your answers?

What did you not like about your answers?

How was the environment?

Figure 15-1

bring up, with whom, and when. Use the worksheet provided to help you make these decisions, and take the opportunity to remember them by writing your responses down.

Think also about the topic of negotiation. Have the persons you met with and are about to meet with started negotiating with you? Even if they haven't brought up the topic, the negotiations have already begun. The more you keep that fact in mind, the more ready you will be to identify and discuss any detail placed

Details that Need to Be Considered for Any Job Offer

Consider the following to help you make a decision:

Job Title (corporate and functional):

Starting Salary:

Benefits:

Will this interfere with your long-ago planned (and paid for) trip?

What, if any, travel as a part of the job's responsibility?

Will relocation be required/desired?

If not, how is the commute?

Have you done your due-diligence?

What will the next step be? How many more steps to expect?

What about timing?

What else do you want/need to know?

Is there anyone at this point you want to meet with if these discussions go further?

What about a start date? How much time will you need?

Will the offer be in writing?

Should you ask for any reimbursement for out-of pocket expenses for these meetings? Should you disclose other pending situations?

A sign-on bonus?

Figure 15-2

before you. This is preferable to being caught off-guard. Depending on the position for which you are applying, you might even be knocked from consideration if someone determines that you are lacking in this skill set. Chapter 16 is devoted to the topic of negotiations.

Before leaving the topic of negotiations, let us just say that you should not be willing to commence any negotiations until you have an offer, preferably in writing. Do not agree to start negotiating any sooner. If any of your interviewers has already asked any questions about pay (what you are making or what you want to receive), they are trying to obtain information that will be extremely important to them as they continue increasingly serious discussions with you. For your part, you should be flattered but be careful to take the questions seriously and control what you are willing to disclose at all times.

While you are remembering what transpired at your earlier meeting(s), recall whether you have already completed an employment application. If you have not until now, good. If you already have, it is important for you to recall (unless you were able to retain a copy) what compensation questions were raised. If you were asked what your rate of pay was at your previous places of employment, what did you disclose? If you gave them your salary history, the good news is that they reviewed that information, and since they asked you to go back, they are going to be able to pay what they think you deserve with the knowledge of what you were earning. If they have not addressed the question since and have not referred to that amount until now, that is a very good sign that you are affordable to them.

If the topic has not yet come up and you have yet to complete an application, or if the application they ask you to complete—whenever they decide to do it—asks for "desired salary," just put in the words "flexible" or "open." If they give you an application that asks for your "current or last salary," we would encourage you to avoid providing it if you can do so. The easiest way is to leave the salary information blank and see if they come back to you and ask you to complete the information requested. Sometimes the interviewer does not think to review the application before your meeting. That might mean they were distracted and forgot or (and here is a bit of bad news) the interviewer has already decided not to refer you on so the question is no longer relevant. Nevertheless, leave it blank and hope for the best. If confronted, apologize and say you forgot to provide that data. If the situation comes to this, you will have no choice but to be honest and disclose. However, don't worry because what you are or were being paid is different from what you would like from your next employer, so just leave it at that. By the way, the longer in the process you are able to delay any pay discussion, the more it works in your favor (think disclosure).

Re-research. News Reports/Industry Changes (or Research—Part Two)

Here you need to do some homework. The length and depth to which you can do research will depend on the time and other commitments you have before your next meeting with this potential employer. Ideally, though, regardless of the time you have to conduct your research before the meeting, you should attempt the following and then feel confident with your efforts, especially when they have produced significant results.

Remember, you are not researching for a term paper for school; you are researching your next possible job—the place where you will spend more time than anywhere else for the total duration of your employment (should you decide to accept an offer when extended by them). Do your homework and due diligence to the point that you will be able to speak confidently and knowledgeably but not so much so that you overwhelm the persons with whom you meet. The point here is not to study, study, study, but rather to have sufficient understanding to be aware of recent developments, and understand the marketplace and its competition.

Be current about the values of the key participants. (How are the employees being treated most recently?) What is the total compensation of the most senior players? (The five highest paid are always a matter of public information in all publicly traded companies.) How much stock does each one possess? Who are the members of the board? Who is the accountant that performs their audits? What has been the recent performance of the stock? Any statements that disclose their attitude toward the law? Have stock options recently been revised (usually a sign of poor performance and a board under the influence of the executive management team). Do they have a separate compliance/governance function?

Perform an online search for the organization, as well as the industry it is in, for the most recent developments and information. If you have time, look at the organization's Web site. If you also have time, go to the Web site of its greatest competitors.

Conduct a people search—looking for any information regarding employees (current, past, retired); customers/noncustomers; vendors; and other suppliers.

Primary Questions That You Should Consider Asking

- Who are the next interviews with? Title/responsibilities?
- What information do they possess regarding you and your application?
- What will your objective be? (It will be one of just two—an offer or the next step, which more often than not will mean more interviews.)

Depending on the organization, there will be one or more additional interviews that you need to complete before an offer is made. Separately or not, there might also be one or more paper tests or work sample tests or some other test (some companies still even use handwriting analysis) that need to be completed before a final decision is made. There might also be a drug test and references to check (don't forget that the exercise of checking references is another form of test which, by the way, is used to screen job candidates in or out).

The key is to maintain your stamina, keep your defenses up, and don't offer any signs of disappointment, impatience—or worse, annoyance with the process or any of the organization's representatives. It will be what it will be. Remember that you too are evaluating the organization to determine whether the closer you get, the better they look.

What Should You Bring?

In Chapter 12, "Last-Minute Checks," there was a review of what you should bring. Once again, you should limit what you take with you. One thing, however, you should be prepared for is an answer to the question "What are you looking for?" Your reply should combine both career opportunity and appropriate compensation. "I am looking for an opportunity to continue my successful career progression at a place where I will continue to be able to make significant contributions while growing professionally." Then they will ask, "What are you hoping to make?" "I would like to be paid fairly and be given a step up from my current pay level."

If they do not follow up with any more questions in this line of inquiry, you should be quiet as well. More likely than not, the next question will be "What are you looking for?" or "Where are you now?" If you keep dodging the question, you will be seen as evasive. So be ready to answer it. Try to just give the base if you feel you are being paid well or competitively. If you feel you have been getting less than what the market is paying, then give your total compensation.

To be sure you are answering correctly, use the worksheet provided in Chapter 16 (Figure 16-3). Prepare for this discussion by writing down the total value of your additional areas of compensation so that you can accurately determine your total annual compensation value. It is for you to know and not to share with others. If you are offered the job, then it might be appropriate if the offer has come in low for you to show exactly what numbers you have been earning. To gain credibility, it would be appropriate to share those numbers using that sheet of paper, but we do not suggest that you share that sheet of paper before you get a definite offer.

As part of your preparation for your follow-up interview, consider putting together a list of references. Delay here for as long as you can because you do not want your references to be contacted unless an offer has already been made or is about to. You need to protect your references so they will not quickly tire by requests for information from them. Secondly, think of yourself and your reputation if your references are repeatedly being sought and you continue to be without a job.

Consider whether there are any articles or other materials that you have either written or otherwise created or that refer to you. And, if you are creative, depending on your area of expertise, you should always have your portfolio with you to save time and let your creative work speak on your behalf. Recall the old saying that one picture is worth a thousand words.

Time to Rehearse

Last, be sure to take some of the limited time you have to rehearse in preparation for the meeting. We do not suggest that you memorize responses yet at the same time you should spend some time reviewing the questions they are likely to ask and your responses should serve as an effective part of your preparation. Recall the position, review the job description and your notes, and practice, practice, practice.

Do Not Forget to Relax

Finally, as we said at the start of the chapter, remember that you should be excited and delighted with the prospect of another round of interviews because your invitation to return is a very positive response to your earlier presentation. Remember it and reflect on it because that should give you additional confidence at the meetings you are about to have.

That said, do not overprepare. Use your instincts to know when to quit and get a good night's rest so that you will be able to interview at your best. (See Figure 15-3.)

Last-Minute Checklist

Key points to review for follow-up interviews

☐ What is the job? Do you have a written job description?

☐ Whom are you to meet with? (correct spelling of name, title)

☐ Contact information?

☐ What was the treatment like that you received last time?

☐ Directions? Is the location easy to get to? How long did it take last time?

☐ Any news developments since last visit?

☐ Did anyone provide any clues about what must-haves anyone hired will need?

☐ What do you think they liked about you and your background?

☐ What do they feel will be a reach?

☐ Do you need (did you promise) to bring anything? Portfolio? Clippings? Recent articles?

☐ Remember to pack several copies of your resume.

☐ Are there any questions that you would like/need answered?

☐ What will you say if any questions are raised regarding salary or compensation?

Figure 15-3

CHAPTER SIXTEEN

Negotiating and Accepting the Offer or Moving on to the Next Interview

Take a moment to bask in your own glory. You either already received a job offer or are just about to get one. Be careful, though. This is not the time to relax—not yet anyway—even though the offer stage is the one you want to get to. You need to consider what items you feel have not been discussed and what you want to do to negotiate. This step gives you one more opportunity to be sure that the job you seek is being offered to you in the way that it should. To be sure that it is, you need to determine what you can and should do. Throughout the negotiation stage keep reminding yourself that this opportunity is also the last chance you have to obtain feedback and confirmation that this is the job you should accept.

For starters, remember that your potential employer is interested in making an offer that best suits its needs. You need to be (and your employer expects you to be) the advocate for your own interests. For you to define the difficult and challenging "fine line" between what you should and shouldn't ask for is key. An unwillingness to ask will result in obtaining less than what you might have otherwise received. What makes this phase particularly troublesome is that most of us prefer not to face it and act. But beware: To not act is operating at one's own peril. And beware of accepting a job offer that includes no opportunity for negotiation.

Getting a Written or Verbal Offer

In case there is any doubt about whether you should get any job offer in writing, let's remove it right away. Always get an offer in writing wherever possible. (Remember: It never hurts to ask. Keep this negotiating tip in mind for all requests, including this one.) We will also agree up front that getting an offer in writing is not always possible. In some industries, it is more commonly accepted than others. Entertainment companies, for instance, are used to giving their key staff members (which might include on-air talent) written contracts, so it is more likely that they would give offer letters, too.

Two comments if your potential employer refuses: Determine the reason they don't want to put it in writing, and consider how much their offer is to be believed.

One reason for asking for the offer in writing is to see if they are willing to give you a written commitment. It is odd when an organization won't do it. Lawyers, for a fee, are always available to employers and are ready to include all the legal language that they can to state in writing that any offer is in no way to be construed as a contract. Frequently, organizations have attorneys employed as staff members available to provide assistance in the drafting of these letters—or a template—whenever the situation warrants.) So if the paper the offer is written on is not a contract, then why should anyone ever be hesitant to put whatever the employer is promising (but nonbinding) in writing?

Also, asking for an offer in writing gives the applicant an excuse to delay a response. "Will this be confirmed in writing? Good. As soon as I have had a chance to review it, you will receive my response." This also provides one more opportunity for due diligence. How long is it taking you to receive the written confirmation? How was it sent? Does it contain what you had been told orally? Is it error free?

Obviously, when you receive the written offer, the answer to the questions raised above will give you additional information about the level of ease with which the organization is able to execute a decision once made and the importance it places on its hiring efforts. We know of one instance where a written offer to a vice president was promised and the candidate was told the offer had been sent by messenger (it was), but it took him two days to receive it.

As a backup, if you are not being given a confirmation in writing, be sure to demonstrate that you are taking notes in front of the person making the offer to reduce the potential for disagreement over terms afterwards. There continue to be instances where the candidate is required to respond to an offer on the spot, but more on that later.

What Should Be Covered in the Offer?

Below is a list of items that always need to be included in any offer. Consider all of the following areas.

Basics (Must Haves)

The following is a list of items that should absolutely be in the offer. If they are not included, ask for an additional letter that spells out the specific terms for each of these areas.

Start Date/Time   Take nothing for granted. What is the specific date and time they wish you to start your new job? If it isn't in writing, be sure to confirm with your written response (see below for other items to include in your response).

Title   This might be in two parts. Your corporate title and, if different, your functional title. There might be more than one title when, for instance, as a sales person, the designation "Executive III" would mean nothing to the outside world, but Vice President for this job is not acceptable internally.

Starting Rate of Pay   Needless to say, this is the primary reason for getting the offer in writing. Review carefully each word. The more complicated the wording, the more careful you need to be. If you still are uncertain of the meaning and/or intent, be sure to discuss the item until it becomes clear. If bonus eligibility and incentive awards are provided either directly in the body of the letter or as an attachment, be sure that what you had discussed during your meetings is now included in writing, without discrepancy.

Name of Supervisor   Confirm that who you thought you would be reporting to is actually the one named in the letter and that the title has not changed.

Location   Obtain specifics as to where you are to initially appear on you first day. First impressions are lasting.

Confirmation Required (or Not)   Be sure to review what is required to be done upon receipt of the letter. If it needs to be signed, review the wording. If the letter is not a contract, then your confirmation that you are accepting the job offered will not be construed as a contract. However, you have accepted the job, and if something better comes along you are not legally or morally able to accept another offer.

The Following Might Also Be Included

The following items might be agreed upon during the course of your negotiations. Be sure all items discussed during the interview process are included in writing as part of the agreement.

Sign-on Bonus   Some organizations give bonuses just for accepting the job offer. It never hurts to ask for one. Find out before your meeting what is done in this industry and what the reputation is for paying sign-on bonuses at the organization you are considering joining. If you have no other items to discuss (although that is rare), then raise this one anyway. Be prepared also to give an amount if asked. Be ready to find out the terms of payment and when it is vested. (If you get fired, you don't want to have to pay it back.) This might be particularly helpful if relocation is involved. Moves do not usually cover everything, so anything additional helps.

Benefits Eligibility   When do they start? If there is any delay and you are paying COBRA premiums, determine what, if any, arrangements the employer is willing to provide as an "offset." If there is a flexible benefit arrangement, see if the COBRA premiums could be paid directly (then at least you will be paying on a pretax basis). Be open to a meeting with an in-house HR expert if it is suggested that you do so (or you might make the offer). Welcome the chance to begin to build relationships before you even start work. One more person to add to your due diligence process. Other benefits to review, by category, include:

- 401(k) and other retirement plans
- Dental
- Vision
- EAP (Employee Assistance Program)
- Disability coverage
- Corporate contribution match
- Tuition refund

Time-Off Policy   What is your current time-off entitlement? Is there room to ask for the same amount that you earned at your last/current employer? Be careful with this one. If you are being paid a premium either in base or with incentives or other payments, the organization that just made you the offer might not be pleased with a request here. At the same time, be sure you understand what is being offered, especially if they talk in terms of PTO (personal time off). First, if they mention PTO, ask them to explain it. Briefly, it is an approach to time off that lumps all your time-off entitlement into one bundle. As part of the policy you usually are paid (in some states required) for any days accumulated that you did not take when you resign. Use Figure 16-1 to determine the total number of days you could receive.

Review your current/most recent arrangement to see how the offer compares. If you get two personal days, three weeks of vacation, and six sick days at your current job, PTO would bundle these three categories. Your total current entitlement should compare with their policy and offer. (They might make an exception at least for the first year, if asked. See the example below.) Keep in mind that most organizations have a "use it or lose it" approach to sick and personal days, meaning unused days cannot be carried forward from one year to the next. Don't be alarmed if your total (no doubt due to the sick day portion) exceeds the arrangement you would receive with your new employer. Make a point of mentioning that they provide a reduced time off allotment even if you are not interested in negotiating for more. (It is usually wise to look elsewhere to be "made whole.") You should bring the topic up, and be sure to mention it if you don't intend to negotiate for more time off. "Even though the time-off allotment is less than what I am eligible for with my current employer, I don't get to take it all anyway, so I am willing to accept it as is. With that in mind, though, I wonder if…." This is an opportunity to obtain something in exchange for the point that you just conceded instead of just letting it go away without obtaining something in return.

Performance Management Program   If you haven't done so already, try to get a job description at this time. It is late in the process, though, so try to avoid being the one to ask. Instead, ask about the performance management program. "How will I be evaluated and at what frequency? May I see a copy of the performance appraisal form?" At that point, ask if there is a current job description if one still has not been offered.

Incentive Eligibility   Find out if your position is eligible for participation in any incentive programs. That might range from an organizationwide profit-sharing plan to individual quarterly goal payouts. By asking, you will know if you are eligible for additional compensation, and the employer will be impressed with your interest in obtaining information regarding your own performance.

Time-Off Entitlement Worksheet

Category	Current/ Most Recent Job	Job Under Consideration
Total Days Annual Vacation		
Personal Days per Year		
Sick Days		
PTO Comparison Subtotal		
Also:		
Total Annual Holidays Observed		
Bereavement Leave Allowance		
Max. Maternity/ Paternity Leave Days		
Max. Jury Duty Days Paid		
Total Annual Military Leave		
Marriage Leave Days		
Is there a Sabbatical allowed?		
Any other days allowed (indicate below)		
Total Time-Off Entitlement		

Figure 16-1

Relocation Details Ask for a copy of the company's relocation policy and procedures. If they do not have one available, ask for a meeting with the department/person responsible. As with benefits, you might have the opportunity to meet one or more persons before you start, allowing you to commence a relationship with the person you are going to rely on for a swift and hassle-free move. If you have pets that need a temporary home, be sure to mention it if you haven't already.

Spouse/Significant Other Considerations If there is a relocation involved, what can the employer do for your spouse/significant other in terms of finding a new job and getting acclimated?

Other Extraordinary Issues You Might Want to Discuss

- *An office.* Not that they won't give you one, but don't take it for granted that they will AND what will it look like? Where is it located?
- Furniture and furnishings. Can you see them?
- *Company car.* If it should be an issue.
- *Additional equipment and services.* Do you need a cell phone? A Blackberry or other Personal Data Assistant?
- *Health/golf club memberships.* Are they offered at your level?
- *Perquisites.* Mention any other items that you feel ought to be part of your job but that have not been discussed before now. (For example, what assistance is available to you?)

See Figure 16-2 for a worksheet to ensure that nothing falls between the cracks to your annoyance later. Remember, assume nothing with the details of the offer. If you did not raise an issue, what you end up getting (or not) will be a decision that remains with your new employer.

How to Consider the Offer

We suggest a basic, simple approach. Make a list with two columns: "This is what I currently have" and "This is what they are offering." Commit it to paper. Use Figure 16-3 for help.

Complete and review Figure 16-3 very carefully. There will more likely be trade-offs. You need to determine which aspects of

Every Offer Will Include:

<u>Must haves:</u>

Category: **Details:**

Start Date

Start Time

Title (Functional)

Title (Corporate, if different)

Rate of Pay at Start

Any Promised Pay Change/Date

Overtime eligibility, if nonexempt

Supervisor's Name/Title

Location

Procedure if confirmation required?

<u>May also contain</u> (Circle categories/provide details on Chart 16-3.)

Category

Short-term Incentive(s)	Stock Options	Pension
Long-term Incentives	Employee Stock Purchase Program	401(K) Program
Bonus(es)	Perquisites	Expense Account
Relocation Considerations	Car	Formula for Payment of Commission
Spousal/Significant Other Considerations	Equipment — Cell phone/ Personal Data Assistant/ Blackberry	Telecommunication arrangements (Work out of your home)
Time-off entitlement	Health Insurance	Future office relocation terms
Performance Management Program	Dental Insurance	Support staff assistance
Training program(s)	Vision Insurance	Buy-out considerations
Job Description	Prescription Drugs	Any others

Figure 16-2

the offer are most important to you. Be sure you have taken everything into consideration.

When to Negotiate and When to Pick Your Battles

Negotiating is an important skill and one that needs to be developed. No one is born knowing how to negotiate (although some take to it so easily that you would think that they were).

Must haves versus "Want to Haves" versus "Throwaways"
First, prepare a list of what items you want to raise, then break them into three categories. Note that the throwaways are for you to concede in an effort to devote more attention to other items that are more important to you. For instance, medical insurance coverage might be unnecessary for you at this time, so you don't really care what you are expected to pay in premiums for coverage. Because of this, though, and the savings to your employer, this might be exchanged for a slight increase in base pay.

Devote your preparation time to determining what the must haves are. These are the potential deal breakers, so think carefully about what items you decide to place in this category.

How to Set up a Win-Win Situation   The goal in negotiations is not to win at the expense of the other person. The objective is to seek an agreement that is acceptable to both parties. If this does not occur and the employer feels had, then the employment arrangement might be still born and it will just be a question of when you will leave. If you feel you were not treated fairly, then you will commence employment with this dark cloud overhead, and it will be a matter of time before the rain starts to fall in the form of your persistent, increasing disenchantment.

To get a win-win negotiation in place, you need to start with you. From the start, you need to agree that the only approach available for you and your potential employer is to see that each has a valid point of view and both are determined to reach a mutually beneficial agreement. There is no room for a win-lose option.

How to Raise Your Issues   Start by numbering them. If you say, "I have three issues," then don't raise four or two. You are locked in, so live with it; the only exception is if the issue you raise then

Offer Comparisons

Category:	What I Have Now	The Offer Includes
Sign-on Bonus		
First Year Base Pay Total		
Short-term Incentives?		
Long-term Incentives?		
Profit Sharing?		
Any other first year payments?		
Equipment, vehicle, other payments-in-kind/ perquisites		
Health & Welfare Benefits:		
— Health, Dental, Vision		
— Disability — Short term		
—Disability — Long term		
Life Insurance		
Accidental Death & Dismemberment		
Business Travel Accident		
Retirement Benefits Defined Benefit (Traditional Pension)		
Defined Contribution (401(K) Plan)		
Time-off entitlement (take from 16-2)		
Tuition Refund		
Employee Assistance Program		
Matching Contributions to Charities and Educational Institutions		
Other Benefits Not Mentioned Elsewhere		

Figure 16-3

becomes part of a larger issue. For example, "The base you offer is less than my current rate of pay, so I have a request that I hope you are willing to accept. You will allow me to work from home one day each week." If this catches your potential employer off guard, he might come back and say, I can't do that but I will allow you to ...." That in turn might cause you to raise something else that was not part of your original group of issues.

When raising issues, remember to:

- Have them identified in advance. Reflect on what the response might be and then, in turn, on what your reply ought to be.
- Number them—"I have three." Once you say the number stick with it unless they will agree that your list may be changed due to the impact of an item raised.
- Be careful not to have too many.
- Identify them specifically. Break them down into must haves, want to haves, and throwaways.
- At all costs, avoid dealing with issues that are too small for the level of the position that is under consideration.
- Determine their order. One obvious approach, once you have decided to accept is to address throwaways first, must haves second, and nice-to-haves last.
- Know when to stop. It is not over till it's over, but when it is, it is.
- Assume nothing.

One More Scenario to be Prepared For

What if you are not allowed to leave without a decision?

This is a tough situation, and the decision on how to handle it needs to be yours. There are reasons to simply accept the job before leaving your interview. First, though, be careful and don't give up. Determine the reason they wish you to give an immediate response. Second, even though they say they want an immediate response, you still might ask them to allow you to think about it overnight with a promise "to get back to them no later than 10 AM tomorrow." You might even add, "I am grateful and appreciate the swiftness of your offer, however I need to complete [an assignment...or two or three. Watch what you say and don't share too many details regarding your current activities]."

Consider whether you want to continue negotiating before you decide. Here is an example of a powerful response:

> Thanks so much for your offer. I have no problem giving you a response before my departure. Let me ask you though when will I receive the offer in writing. [They might have it right there and then.] I also would like to raise two [or whatever number of items that you plan to raise] issues that I hope will be part of the package.

You then, of course, need to have those two issues ready for discussion and need to be decisive if they meet your requests without hesitation:

> I have already committed to a trip from ___ to ___ before we started our discussions. "Will I be able to have the time off?" Do not add "...I don't expect to get paid." Consider whether you want to offer the phrase later after hearing their response. Remember they might offer to pay you for the time.

Always have some item ready for negotiating in anticipation of this situation. Once you accept, the negotiation stops. An easy and obvious opportunity is a discussion of benefits. When do they start?

> I need to ensure that there is a coordination in effect. "Will you be willing to reimburse me for my COBRA expenses until I am covered here?"

Or:

> Is there any flexibility regarding the time off I will be eligible to receive? You offer 16 days PTO (personal time off) per year. At my current employer, I now am eligible for three weeks of vacation each year. Can anything be done so that I am "made whole?"

This request might not be possible, but it might give you a reason to see if something can be done elsewhere, such as increasing the base or a sign-on bonus or additional time off the first year.

It's a great opportunity if you ask for something, and they need to get back to you. You really have won if they want an immediate reply but can't say whether there is any opportunity to give in to any of your requests. It gives you more time to consider the offer. Even if you say yes, and they take a hard stand, you could always reconsider and walk away.

A Word about Recruiters

If you have a recruiter who is going to be paid for your successful placement, keep her in the negotiation loop. Raise the issues through her (unless you decide the recruiter is more interested in collecting the fee than attending to your requests). Effective recruiters realize that for a successful placement, they need a successful win-win negotiation. She will see you through each of the items that you seek. If the negotiations seem a losing battle, you need to determine whether the recruiter truly understands the limitations of her employer client or if she just does not want to raise these issues. In those circumstances, you need to take responsibility for the process and determine to what extent you wish to pursue directly with your potential employer.

When You Must Move On

Reality Check—Taking Stock of Offer/Nonoffer and Your Candidacy

You owe it to yourself to not accept just any offer but instead to accept only those that are a wise choice. In a tough job market where you read about statistics that indicate to get any offer you must go through at least 20 different interviews, how can you choose to pass and start all over? For starters, the worst thing you can do is accept a job that you really do not want. Consider the following.

Is the Job Realistic for You? Do You Really Want It? A big question. The last thing you want to do, after all your effort, is accept the wrong job and have to go through a job search all over again. Be sure you are agreeing to join an organization for all the right reasons. Remember, you spend more time at your job than you do at any other activity, including sleeping.

If You Did Not Get an Offer, Why Not? Could you have done anything to change the outcome? Review as much as you can remember about each step in the process, paying particular attention to the last ones to try to determine what it was that you could (or could not have) done differently. Were the reasons you were dropped from consideration beyond your control?

Always Have Plan B and Plan C

As much as we hate to mention it, the truth is that even with a written offer in hand, two negative things can still take place. The offer can be withdrawn or rescinded. What is the difference? In these turbulent times and ever-changing marketplace, organizations sometimes change direction suddenly and without anticipation. In these situations, it is possible that the new direction the organization is embarking on is one that includes the elimination of the position that was to be filled by you. In this situation you will be told that the position is no longer available and is withdrawn. It unfortunately happens sometimes between the time the offer is extended and accepted and the new employee's start date. In one extreme situation, a relocated new hire learned of the elimination of his job by reading the *Wall Street Journal* on his way to his first day of work.

An offer is *rescinded* if the offer is given to you and upon executing due diligence your potential employer determines that the information obtained regarding your background and/or experience is damaging to your employment. The offer may then bewithdrawn, and you are told in words to that effect. You must have a backup plan in case either of these things occurs.

What Other Leads Have You Been Juggling?   Keep pursuing any other job opportunities until you are actually starting to work—right up to the time you report to your new job and even afterward, just to be safe. Remember that you have put a lot of effort into your job search (and planted a lot of seeds in the process), and therefore it would be foolish to just shut everything down. Are we suggesting that your job search in this economy is a never-ending process? That is exactly what we are suggesting. We certainly don't encourage you to continue searching for a job in the same persistent way you did when it was your full-time effort. Simply put, you just don't have the time. At the same time, if any of the feelers you sent out starts to show a yield, follow up.

Two Last Items

Give a Written Response—Whether You Accept the Offer or Not

Always put your acceptance or rejection of the offer in writing. This is the professional way to respond, and one more opportunity to demonstrate how lucky they are to have you (or how unfortunate that you did not accept the offer). Send it to the person you feel is most responsible for your offer, and be sure to include a copy for your contact in HR, if that is not the person to whom the letter is addressed.

If You Are Accepting the Offer

If you accept the offer, be sure that you confirm the start date details. Mention if you are submitting a signed copy of their letter. Be sure to identify any items that were not mentioned in the written offer. If there is no other discussion or correspondence before you start, you should mention your letter and the lingering issues as soon as you can on day one. You need to determine if the item(s) is (are) deal breakers. (See Figure 16-4.)

Last-Minute Checklist
Negotiating Tips

☐ You need to want to negotiate.

☐ Everything is negotiable.

☐ Never negotiate before you get an offer, preferably in writing.

☐ Always negotiate more than one issue, ideally no less than three.

☐ Break your issues down into three groups: "must-haves," "nice to haves," and "throwaways."

☐ Think "win-win."

☐ Know when to stop.

Figure 16-4

CHAPTER SEVENTEEN

Summary

A Fourth R for Good Measure

If you have come this far and you still have not had your interview, it cannot be too far away.

At this point, you have already done everything that you were able to in your efforts to be successful at the interview. You have done as much as you could with the time that you had available to you. We even warned you not to overprepare.

As for the three Rs, with your research complete, you have gone through your Rehearsal. Now it is time once more to Relax and look at a fourth R. You are Ready!

You Are Ready

You are now ready to go and face this very exciting opportunity. You do not know if you will be successful, and it might take a while to determine your results by that measure. Lao Tsu is quoted to have said, "A thousand-mile journey begins with a single step."

You do not know what is ahead for you. Be delighted with the fact that you have this meeting, but do not make the visit solely an opportunity for the organization to evaluate you. The job search is about you and what it is you want to do as the next step in your career, as well as where you want to do it.

Remember as you go through the interview to keep a sharp ear tuned as much to what is said as to what is not said. Take advantage and keep your eyes wide open to all that you see on your visit. Each hallway, office, reception area, and parking lot is one more venue for you to gain insight into the organization and to help determine whether it is the place where you can devote the greatest portion of your time.

Good luck!

INDEX

Note: **Boldface** numbers indicate illustrations.

Index

About the Authors

Matt and **Nanette DeLuca** are the authors of the bestsellers *Best Answers to the Most Frequently Asked Interview Questions* and *More Best Answers to the 201 Most Frequently Asked Interview Questions.* Matt is a principal at the Management Resource Group, a human resources consulting, training, and recruiting company.